FORTRESS · 106

FORTS OF THE WAR OF 1812

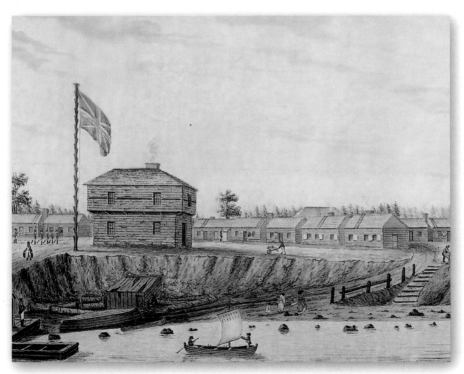

RENÉ CHARTRAND ILLUSTRATED BY DONATO SPEDALIERE

Series editor Marcus Cowper

First published in 2012 by Osprey Publishing
Midland House, West Way, Botley, Oxford OX2 0PH, UK
44-02 23rd St, Suite 219, Long Island City, New York 11101, USA

E-mail: info@ospreypublishing.com

ISBN: 978 1 84908 576 2
E-book ISBN: 978 1 84908 577 9

Editorial by Ilios Publishing Ltd, Oxford, UK (www.iliospublishing.com)
Cartography: Map Studio, Romsey, UK
Page layout by Ken Vail Graphic Design, Cambridge, UK (kvgd.com)
Typset in Myriad and Sabon
Index by Marie-Pierre Evans
Originated by United Graphics Pte Ltd
Printed in China through Bookbuilders

12 13 14 15 16   10 9 8 7 6 5 4 3 2 1

Osprey Publishing are supporting the Woodland Trust, the UK's leading woodland conservation charity, by funding the dedication of trees.

www.ospreypublishing.com

DEDICATION

When finishing his research visit to Fort McHenry, the author witnessed from afar a moving scene. It was the early evening of a beautiful day and the empty fort was being closed by his very kind colleague, historian Scott Sheads of the National Park Service's fort staff, when a little boy – he was perhaps five – accompanied by his parents and grandparents walked in. Scott was about to hoist the night version of the national flag, somewhat smaller than the daytime one, but still impressively large. The little boy was invited by Scott to "help" raise the flag and the boy keenly took and pulled the rope. As the Star Spangled Banner rose, the proud parents started singing the national anthem, soon joined by all. The beauty of this moment, at the very spot that inspired the anthem's words during the tragic night of September 13, 1814, defies description. This humble work is dedicated to that little American boy.

ACKNOWLEDGEMENTS

I would like to most kindly thank Scott Sheads of Fort McHenry in Maryland, Brian Dunnigan of Michigan, Don Graves of Ontario, and the many helpful colleagues at the National Historic Sites of Parks Canada, Library and Archives Canada in Ottawa, The National Archives of the United Kingdom in Kew, and the Library of Congress in Washington. Unless otherwise credited, all photographs are by the author.

ARTIST'S NOTE

Readers may care to note that the original paintings from which the color plates in this book were prepared are available for private sale. All reproduction copyright whatsoever is retained by the Publishers. All enquiries should be addressed to:

Alina Illustrazioni, C. S. Montecchio, San Lorenzo 234, 52044, Cortona Arezzo, Italy

The Publishers regret that they can enter into no correspondence upon this matter.

THE FORTRESS STUDY GROUP (FSG)

The object of the FSG is to advance the education of the public in the study of all aspects of fortifications and their armaments, especially works constructed to mount or resist artillery. The FSG holds an annual conference in September over a long weekend with visits and evening lectures, an annual tour abroad lasting about eight days, and an annual Members' Day.

The FSG journal FORT is published annually, and its newsletter Casemate is published three times a year. Membership is international. For further details, please contact:
secretary@fsgfort.com
Website: www.fsgfort.com

THE HISTORY OF FORTIFICATION STUDY CENTER (HFSC)

The History of Fortification Study Center (HFSC) is an international scientific research organization that aims to unite specialists in the history of military architecture from antiquity to the 20th century (including historians, art historians, archeologists, architects and those with a military background). The center has its own scientific council, which is made up of authoritative experts who have made an important contribution to the study of fortification.

The HFSC's activities involve organizing conferences, launching research expeditions to study monuments of defensive architecture, contributing to the preservation of such monuments, arranging lectures and special courses in the history of fortification and producing published works such as the refereed academic journal Questions of the History of Fortification, monographs and books on the history of fortification. It also holds a competition for the best publication of the year devoted to the history of fortification.

The headquarters of the HFSC is in Moscow, Russia, but the Center is active in the international arena and both scholars and amateurs from all countries are welcome to join. More detailed information about the HFSC and its activities can be found on the website: www.hfsc.3dn.ru
E-mail: ciif-info@yandex.ru

CONTENTS

FORTS OF THE WAR OF 1812

INTRODUCTION

Following the end of the American War of Independence, the eastern part of North America was divided between the new United States of America and British North America. The United States' rapidly growing population lived mostly near the shores of the Atlantic Ocean, whereas British territory comprised both small colonies on the North Atlantic coast and the enormous territories of Canada and Rupert's Land that extended all the way to the Pacific Ocean, which was reached in 1794 by Montréal fur trader Alexander Mackenzie. The purchase of the huge but sparsely settled French territory of Louisiana by the United States in 1803 expanded its frontiers west of the Mississippi River. US Army explorers Lewis and Clark reached the Pacific in 1805. Spain still had enclaves in the present-day states of Florida, Alabama, and Mississippi, as well as a western domain extending from Texas to California. This was the geopolitical division of North America at the eve of the War of 1812.

With regards to fortifications, North America after 1783 had a peculiar situation. Its vast territories were sprinkled with many forts. The most numerous were the western frontier forts, many of them built by settlers and fur traders, nearly all fairly small and made of wood. The eastern seaboard was also dotted with forts and batteries, some large, but most of a modest size, generally made

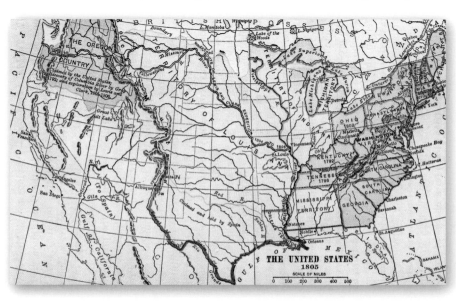

RIGHT
Map of the United States in the early 19th century. It was already a large country for a small regular army to defend. (Private collection)

OPPOSITE
Urban centers such as New York, Newport, or Halifax usually had a defensive complex of several forts and batteries. Only the forts that had regular garrisons are shown. There were many temporary forts garrisoned by militias or volunteers.

4

The main forts and towns in North America at the time of the War of 1812

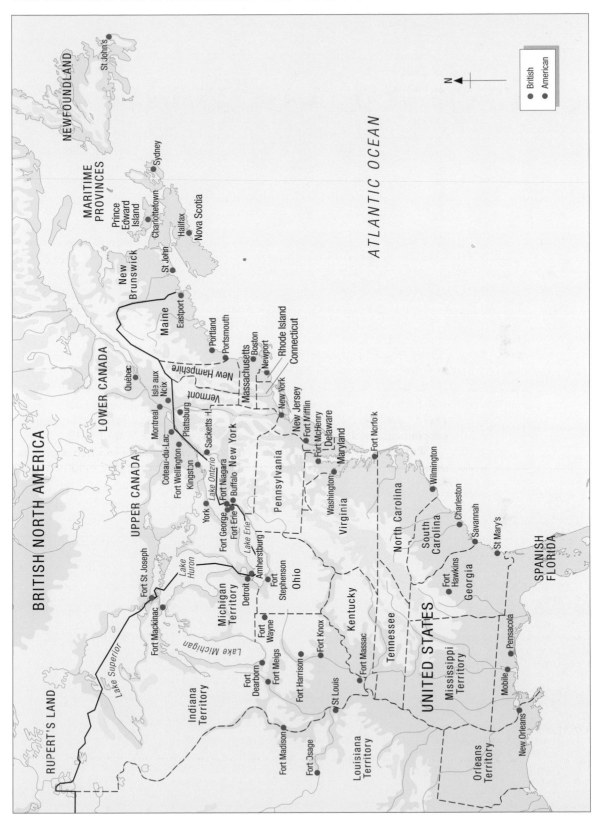

of earth and wood and mounted with artillery because nearly all these fortifications were meant to repel seaborne enemies. There were practically no masonry fortifications or citadels.

There were exceptions, such as the large stone fort of San Marcos in St Augustine, in Spanish Florida. In the British domains, Québec was the only large city in North America that featured redoubtable curtain walls faced with stone. Since Britain enjoyed unrivalled superiority at sea, its core policy concentrated on investing the huge sums required to maintain its fleet as the strongest in the world instead of building extensive coastal fortifications, and this extended to North America. In the nascent United States of the later 1780s and early 1790s, the War of Independence had left its harbors largely defenseless. Even the powerful fortifications guarding Boston and New York City had been ravaged. At that time, the United States did not have a navy and its regular army was minuscule. Now that it was an independent nation, it had to face the responsibility and expense of its own defense.

CHRONOLOGY

Note: in nearly all actions, the term "British" used here includes Canadians and Indians as well as soldiers from the United Kingdom.

1796

February 29	Jay's Treaty between the United States and Britain is signed. American forts and towns still occupied by British forces are turned over to United States troops in compliance with the 1783 treaty.

1812

June 18	United States declares war on Britain.
July 17	British capture Fort Mackinac (also called Fort Michilimackinac).
August 15	Indians allied to the British capture Fort Dearborn (Chicago), Illionis.
August 16	British capture Detroit, Michigan.
November 21	Artillery duel between Fort Niagara, New York, and Fort George, Upper Canada.

1813

February 22	British capture Ogdensburg, New York.
April 27	Americans capture York, Upper Canada (Toronto, Ontario).
April 28 to May 9	British unsuccessful siege of Fort Meigs, Ohio.
May 27	Americans capture Fort George, Upper Canada.
August 2	Americans repulse attack on Fort Stepenson, Ohio.
December 10	Americans evacuate Fort George and burn Newark (now Niagara-on-the-Lake), Upper Canada.
December 19	British capture Fort Niagara, New York.

1814

May 5–6	British capture Oswego, New York.
March 30	British repulse attack on Lacolle, Lower Canada.
July 3	Americans capture Fort Erie, Upper Canada.
July 18	British capture Fort Sullivan at Eastport, Maine.
July 20	British capture Prairie du Chien, Wisconsin.
August & September	British siege of Fort Erie, Upper Canada.
August 4	American attack on Fort Mackinac, Michigan, repulsed.
September 11	Repulse of British attack on Plattsburgh, New York.
September 13	British bombard Fort McHenry, Maryland.
December 24	Treaty of peace signed between American and British representatives at Ghent, Belgium.

1815

January 8–9	Americans repulse British at New Orleans, Louisiana.
February 11	British capture Fort Bowyer, Alabama.

THE UNITED STATES

Fortification systems

During the early years of the American Republic, no one really wanted to think about military matters. As a result, a nation of about four million people had next to no defense establishment at all. What regular-army units there were consisted initially of a couple of companies to guard stores at West Point and the fort at Pittsburgh, augmented after a few years to a mixed battalion of infantry and artillery to keep hostile Indians at bay on the western frontier. There was no army staff to speak of, no engineer corps to build and upkeep fortifications, no military academies to educate future officers, and no navy to protect American ships from pirates. If there was an emergency, the early American defense policy was to call out some of the state militias on active service. Eventually, this situation became worrisome to some Americans, especially from 1789. In that year the French Revolution gradually drew nearly all nations of Europe into a long period of war that would end only in 1815. This brought great instability to world affairs and, by 1793, Britain, Spain, and France, all of whom had territories near the United States, were embroiled in the hostilities. Combat did not occur on the North American mainland, but there was fierce fighting in the West Indies that included fleets attacking fortified cities.

The United States remained neutral, but there could be no doubt that the world outside its borders was not as safe as it had been before 1789. Furthermore, many Indian nations on the northwestern frontier resented the arrival of Americans who were settling in increasing numbers in places that would become the states of Tennessee, Indiana, Kentucky, Ohio, and Michigan. Many settlers were killed during the 1780s, and open warfare broke out in 1790. After suffering a humiliating defeat at the hands of the Indians in November 1791, the regular army was expanded to over 5,000 men and, with the help of state volunteers, crushed the Indians at the battle of Fallen Timbers in August 1794. Several large wooden forts were built in the northwest at that time, notably Fort Washington in 1790, which evolved into the city of Cincinnati, Ohio.

Meanwhile, the safety of American ports was a growing concern. In February 1794 a committee appointed by the House of Representatives to look into the defenses of the east coast's harbors reported on the measures necessary to put 16 ports into "a state of defense… and that the parapets of the batteries and redoubts should be formed of earth" and that these forts "be garrisoned by troops in the pay of the United States." About 200 cannon were needed, along with some 700 troops to be posted in the fortifications. This report was approved and its implementation resulted in what came to be known as the American "First System" of seacoastal fortifications. In most cases the work consisted of repairing and expanding fortifications that were already in place. By 1800 some $620,000, quite a substantial sum at the time, had been spent in the last six years on the forts and batteries of 20 harbors: Portland, Maine; Portsmouth, New Hampshire; Salem, Marblehead, Gloucester, and Boston, Massachusetts; Newport, Rhode Island; New London, Connecticut; New York, New York; Philadelphia, Pennsylvania; Baltimore and Annapolis, Maryland; Norfolk and Alexandria, Virginia; Cape Fear and Bacon Island, North Carolina; Charleston and Georgetown, South Carolina; and Savannah and St Mary's, Georgia.

It was becoming clear that some of the smaller and more isolated places would not be very effective in deterring a large naval raid. Thus, works on such places as Bacon Island were abandoned. Conversely, the large harbors remained largely under-protected. These were economically important trade centers and businessmen as well as local authorities increasingly clamored for more fortifications to protect these ports. At the time of the Quasi-War with France (1798–1800) Boston had only a rickety and badly repaired fort on Castle Island, which had replaced the sturdy masonry citadel that had been destroyed during the American Revolution, and Baltimore could depend only on shore batteries. Fort Jay and some batteries had been built in New York City, and Fort Mifflin had been extensively rebuilt at Philadelphia, but much more needed to be done.

To address these issues, not only was much more money needed to build large new forts, but a reorganization in the army that favored engineering and artillery was necessary. A first step was made in recognizing that engineering was a component in the new title of the "Corps of Artillerists and Engineers" in May 1794, but with the notion that engineers were considered "more as civil than military" officers. Indeed, civilian architects were at times retained to design fortifications. The corps had very few officers who had formal education as engineers or as artillerymen, and these were all Frenchmen. Nevertheless, hard work and ingenuity were displayed by all. Earthen forts and batteries that were as well designed and built as anywhere else appeared on the outskirts of American coastal cities.

In time, it became recognized that the duties of artillerymen and engineers, while they complemented each other, were nevertheless distinct; the question of professional training for future engineer officers also had to be solved. This latter aspect was important not only for the army, but for the country as a whole. There was then no specialized engineering school in the United States and the first civil-engineering degrees in the nation were granted only from the 1830s. On March 16, 1802, President Thomas Jefferson was given authority by Congress to organize the United States Corps of Engineers and a military academy that the corps would supervise. The headquarters of both the corps and the academy was at West Point, New York. Beginnings were modest, the corps initially having only seven officers and ten cadets. By June 1812 this had been raised to 22 officers, 113 non-commissioned officers and artificers, and some 250 cadets, and this remained the corps' establishment through the war. For much of the first half of the 19th century, the corps' work centered largely on the construction of coastal fortifications.

With a worsening international situation in the early years of the 19th century, the safety of American harbors was an ongoing concern. There were increasing tensions with Britain, which had become the undisputed master of the seas after it crushed the Franco-Spanish fleet at Trafalgar in October 1805. In June 1807, off Norfolk, Virginia, the British HMS *Leopard* opened fire on the American frigate USS *Chesapeake*, which had refused to be searched for Royal Navy deserters, provoking the surrender of the *Chesapeake*. This incident outraged the American public and, in 1808, Congress voted to expand the army and the navy and made funds available to build new coastal fortifications as well as to improve those already in place. Officials had already come up with a new fortification plan, which was approved in January and became known as the "Second System" of 1808. Over 50 localities were identified as needing fortifications, but in fact, like in 1794, efforts were concentrated on the more important and vital harbors, especially those of New York City and Boston. All the same, there was work going on in various ways all along the seaboard with over $3,000,000 being spent during the following five years.

In terms of design, the bastioned pentagon and the star layout were favored in the late 18th and early 19th centuries, as seen with Baltimore's Fort McHenry and Boston's Fort Independence. By 1807, a radically different design – which called for a large turret-shaped thick-walled structure that featured several layers of heavy gun batteries – was introduced by United States Corps of Engineers Lieutenant-Colonel Jonathan Williams with the construction in New York City of what soon became known as "Castle Williams," situated on Governors Island close to Fort Jay and facing Manhattan Island. The emphasis was now increasingly made on the primary importance of firepower, a concept brought out by French engineer Marc René de Montalembert (1714–1800) in his *La Fortification perpendiculaire*, which had been gaining adherents since the 1780s. For coastal fortifications, it was reasoned that a structure with very thick masonry walls featuring many guns protected within its galleries and casemates was superior to any wooden ship-of-the-line that would come within its range. This concept also gave rise to the smaller Martello towers that also became popular, especially with British engineers. It also applied to smaller forts, whose layout consisted mainly of a semi-circular battery, a remarkable example of which was built from 1809 at Norforlk, Virginia.

With the Second System, American fortifications attained an enviable "state-of-the-art" status that made some of them among the most modern and potentially lethal in the world. This was especially true of the Second System forts in New York, which made the city's harbor defenses practically invulnerable to any hostile ships. Indeed, as will be seen below, even a First System fort such as Baltimore's Fort McHenry prevailed under attack by an enemy squadron. It can be safely argued that only very secondary seacoast ports could be successfully attacked, which is what occurred during the War of 1812.

Frontier forts were very different, and nowhere near as much funding was ever devoted to these wooden stockade structures; they were viewed as only temporary. Many of them were built by militiamen and settlers of the western frontier states. Their design tended to be quite simple, often incorporating lodgings as part of a wall, as in colonial times. Larger fortifications tended to be rectangular works, whose curtain walls were dotted with large blockhouses. Examples from the War of 1812 include Fort Meigs, Ohio, and Plattsburgh, New York.

There were hundreds of stockade forts and blockhouses along the western frontier and dozens of small seacoast batteries and occasional blockhouses all along the coast, nearly all of which were erected by local communities. These might have been garrisoned by local militiamen in times of emergency, but otherwise would not have had a garrison. In this short study, we concentrate mainly on the forts that were built by the United States government and garrisoned by regular troops. These fortifications tended to be the more strategically important ones.

Boston and New England

Starting in the north, Boston with its population of about 40,000 inhabitants was the most obvious major target for a fleet sailing from Halifax. In colonial times, Massachusetts had built the very powerful masonry Castle William on Castle Island, which commanded the narrow entrance to the harbor. However, the fort had been largely destroyed by the British Army when it evacuated Boston in 1776. The Americans had repaired it as best as they could during the War of Independence, the resulting earthworks being neglected after 1780. In 1785 it became a penitentiary. Castle Island being the key to Boston's harbor, it was identified in 1794 as a location in the First System of fortifications, but less than $2,000 of federal funds was spent on repairs in the next two years and nothing thereafter.

It was renamed Fort Independence in August 1799, and a small garrison was posted there, a year after the island had been transferred to federal authority. The authorities had concluded that an entirely new and quite large fort had to be built on Castle Island to effectively secure the harbor. Construction started in 1800. Designed by Jean Fontin, an engineer of French origin, it consisted of a masonry pentagon with five large bastions that could hold up to 42 cannon. Initially, two outside batteries of six guns in front of the walls made any enemy approach a dangerous undertaking. The fort had cost $184,000 by the time it was completed in 1803. Most guns were placed on the curtain walls facing the water. This was only the first part of the plan to protect the harbor. Shortly after the Chesapeake incident, Bostonians must have been reassured when, in 1808,

Governors Island and Castle Island, Boston harbor. Although of the late 19th century, this detail from a map of a bird's-eye view of Boston has the advantage of showing the outlines of the site of the two main guardians of Boston harbor during the War of 1812: Fort Warren on Governors Island and Fort Independence on Castle Island. Murderous crossfire across the harbor's only entrance could be effected with Fort Warren's dozen guns. Fort Independence was the most formidable, being a large masonry pentagon with five bastions boasting over 40 guns, which shape it still has today. (Library of Congress, Washington, DC)

they saw construction work on Governors Island, just north of Castle Island, that evolved into Fort Warren (renamed Fort Winthrop in 1833). This was a "star fort, of masonry, with twelve guns mounted" and on the south point and west end of the island, "semi-circular batteries of masonry" having ten guns each to provide crossfire with Fort Independence. Some 133 men of the US Army were posted in Boston in June 1812.

The New England coast was dotted with small and medium-sized towns, all of which wanted their own citadel. There were thus many small forts and batteries such as "a battery of wood filled with sand, and surmounted with sod" at Newburyport, Massachusetts, according to an 1809 report by Secretary of War Henry Dearborn. Another example was the fort at Marblehead, Massachusetts, later known as Fort Sewall, which had eight guns. Nevertheless, a few of these small works on the coast of Maine were destined to be captured by the British in September 1814, such as "the small battery" of four guns at the village of Machias. Fort Sullivan at Eastport, another small semi-circular earthen battery of four guns, was taken at the same time, and, renamed Fort Sherbrooke, had a British garrison until 1818. Another four-gun battery named Fort Madison at Castine was taken by the British and renamed Fort Castine. Also at Castine was Fort Penobscot, which was occupied, expanded, and renamed Fort George by the British, who occupied these enclaves in northern Maine without much fighting and then carried on a thriving trade with Americans now suddenly unimpaired by the Royal Navy's blockade of the United States coast. The profits were such that Nova Scotia businessmen made enough money to fund the opening of Dalhousie University in Halifax after the war, one of the happier results of an otherwise somewhat futile and unnecessary conflict.

In northern Maine, as elsewhere on the coast, forts outside of Boston that had US Army garrisons were few and far between. Farther south in Maine, one of these was Fort Edgecomb, which was a blockhouse with a battery surrounded by earthworks, built in 1808 at Wiscasset. It had a garrison of 44 men of the 4th United States Infantry in late 1811. There were 55 United States Light Artillery gunners posted at Fort Preble, which was "a new [1808] enclosed work of stone and brick masonry" that commanded Portland's harbor entrance. Fort Scammel was "a new work, of similar materials" including a blockhouse, sited opposite Fort Preble. Troops would also have occasionally been seen at the Fort Sumner Battery north of Portland.

New Hampshire's Fort Constitution on New Castle Point at the entrance of Portsmouth harbor was on a site that had been fortified since colonial times and which had been rebuilt during 1807–08. At the eve of the war it had some 36 guns, was made "principally of stone masonry," and was garrisoned by some 77 United States Corps of Artillery gunners. Some of them must have also served at Fort McCleary, described in 1809 as "a new strong work of masonry … erected on Kittery Point opposite Fort Constitution," obviously to provide a crossfire upon any hostile ship.

In Massachusetts, two localities had small US Army detachments besides Boston. Some 74 men of the 4th United States Infantry were lodged at the new barracks at Salem's Fort Pickering, an enclosed battery of earth and masonry featuring six guns, and with a brick barracks and a "blockhouse, with a magazine under it," sited on Winter Island in the harbor. Nearby Plum Island had Fort Morrison, a small six-gun semi-circular masonry battery that may have had a detachment of Salem's regulars. There were also 32 troopers of the Light Dragoons at New Bedford, no doubt lodged at the new wooden barracks

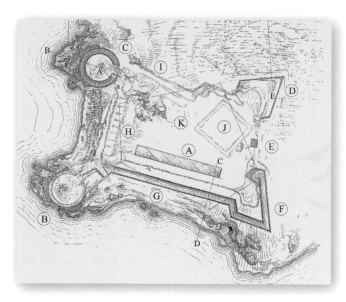

built at the "enclosed work of masonry, mounting six guns, with a brick magazine, and barracks for forty men including officers." It commanded the entrance of the harbor at about 2 miles (3.2km) south of the town, most likely on the site of the present Fort Taber. Fort Sewall at Marblehead was an irregular masonry enclosed battery armed with 13 18-pdr guns, which protected the harbor where the USS *Constitution* was anchored during the war.

The next most important area to secure was the entrance to Rhode Island's Narragansett Bay, which led to Newport and Providence, two of the more important towns in New England. The designers of the First System articulated a remarkable series of forts built from 1798 that submitted the wide and navigable East Entrance to a field of fire from the coast artillery. Coming into the bay, enemy ships would first come within the range of a large masonry oval tower fort, which was an elevated battery built on a point called The Dumplings on the western side. The entrance being wide, Fort Adams was built to cover the entrance from the eastern side with a dozen guns. Furthermore, as ships would move into the bay, they would come within range of Fort Hamilton on Rose Island to the north, the main work of the Narragansett Bay defense complex, which had some 40 long-rage guns. Finally, the large battery named Fort Wolcott on Goat Island next to the harbor of Newport provided a field of fire for 18 guns that, at farther distances, crossed with that of forts Hamilton and Adams. In June 1812 nearly 200 men of the US Army were posted in the Newport area to garrison these forts. The forts themselves were designed by Stephane Rochefontaine and Anne Marie Tousard, and presented an extraordinary mixture of just about every new and traditional concept then in vogue. The strong Martello-type tower at The Dumplings was then a revolutionary new design and it was also incorporated as two of the four bastions of Fort Hamilton. Slightly more conventional designs were employed at forts Adams and Wolcott, which nevertheless presented remarkably innovative designs. All of these new and state-of-the-art fortifications made Narragansett Bay a very challenging place to enter by force of arms, and it is a testament to their effectiveness that no enemy ever dared attempt such an action after their construction.

Fort Hamilton on Rose Island near Newport, Rhode Island, c.1798–1815. This remarkable work combined both the new tower concept as well as older bastions. A: bombproof barracks; B: southwest circular bastion; C: northwest circular bastion; D: northeast bastion; E: officers' quarters; F: southeast bastion; G: south curtain wall; H: west rampart; I: north curtain wall; J: French citadel (1780); K: parade. (Plate by Todd A. Croteau based on a plan by Major Anne Louis de Tousard; Library of Congress, Washington, DC)

Two of the four First System works guarding the entrance into Narragansett Bay, Rhode Island. At left is the tower at The Dumplings, a powerful artillery fort built according to the latest theories in coastal defense. At right is Fort Adams, west of Newport, built on an irregular star plan with a large hornwork also laid out in an irregular plan. (Library of Congress, Washington, DC)

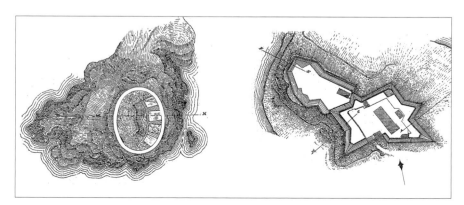

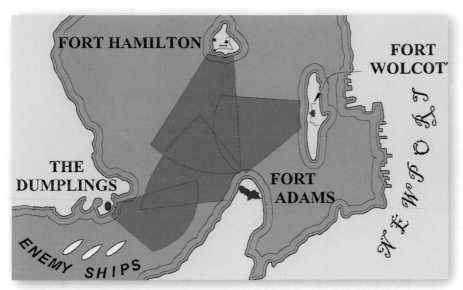

FORT HAMILTON

FORT WOLCOT'

THE DUMPLINGS

FORT ADAMS

NEWPORT

ENEMY SHIPS

In Connecticut, Fort Trumbull in New London was the only fort in that state with a regular garrison, consisting of a company of light dragoons. It was an enclosed work of earth and masonry that could mount some 25 guns. Stonington and New Haven had only small works with four and six guns respectively.

New York City

Possibly the most important harbor to defend on the American coast was that of New York City. The fortifications of the colonial era were inadequate and, by the early 1790s, the largest and richest city in the nation was almost defenseless. The fort originally built by the Dutch at the southern tip of Manhattan Island had been razed and the battery in front of it transformed into a public park named The Battery. Access from the sea into the Hudson River was relatively easy because its estuary was fairly wide, so the defenses of the city would have to rest on the smaller adjoining islands close to Manhattan. Governors Island, just southeast of Manhattan, offered the best site and, from 1794, construction started on Fort Jay, which was originally a "fort made of earth, [with] two batteries under its protection, partly lined with brick masonry." By 1801, that and other minor works consisting of small batteries on Bedoes and Oyster (later Liberty and Ellis) islands had cost $100,000, which was only a little more than one sixth of the entire budget spent on coastal fortifications in the preceding seven years, and it was quite inadequate to secure the city.

In 1805, the Chief Engineer, Lieutenant-Colonel Jonathan Williams, warned Secretary of War Henry

Dearborn that there seemed to be no defense against warships that might attack the city. This very somber assessment was followed by complaints from merchants, who pointed out that one third of the federal government's revenue was collected in New York City, yet its fortifications had been utterly neglected. Congress concurred and, from 1806, Fort Jay was renamed Fort Columbus (until 1904 when its original name was restored) and rebuilt as a large fort that could mount up to 104 guns with four bastions and a ravelin. While Fort Columbus had a conventional Vauban-style design, the other forts built to protect New York City were very different and owed more to the ideas of Montalembert and other revisionists of fortifications architecture. Foremost among these was what became known as Castle Williams, whose construction started in 1807. Lieutenant-Colonel Williams personally took charge of rebuilding the fortifications of New York's inner harbor, which shows that this was now seen as the most urgent work to be done on the nation's coastal defenses. Castle Williams, built close to Fort Columbus on the northwest tip of Governors Island, consisted of a very large casemate that could hold some 80 guns (later increased to 102), the first such structure built in the United States. This radically different type of coastal fort was to strongly influence American coastal defenses for the next half century. Castle Williams had very thick masonry walls that went up four stories, each of which contained powerful batteries of heavy artillery that were almost invulnerable to the fire of enemy warships. In the days of wooden sailing ships, any large man-of-war with hostile intention approaching a fort such as Castle Williams was almost certain to suffer heavy damage or even be sunk, while the fort would likely remain almost unscathed. This would be especially true if the fort's garrison consisted of competent gunners. While there may have been doubts as to the efficiency of the small US Army's infantry, its Corps of Artillery was undoubtedly one of the most professional and learned such forces anywhere, and this made the new and highly innovative forts being built as part of the Second System even more lethal.

A casemated circular fort such as Castle Williams not only offered the possibility of having several tiers of well-protected heavy cannon within its thick walls, but it also did not require a huge garrison and its requirements for land were far less than for a conventional Vauban- or pentagon-style fort. In a city like New York City, where real estate on lower Manhattan was already at a premium, the notion of building powerful forts that did not take up much space was very good news indeed to the business community.

Obviously, Williams was profoundly influenced by Montalembert's ideas, whose works he probably read when he was a young diplomat in Paris between 1776 and 1785, assisting his great-uncle Benjamin Franklin, who was the American ambassador to France. He had also gained a solid theoretical knowledge of the latest trends in fortification designs. Now back in the United States and at the peak of his professional ability, being also responsible for the West Point Military

Castle Williams in New York City, c.1815. This remarkable and imposing masonry fort with its three levels of gun batteries made it a formidable obstacle for any hostile ship approaching New York's harbor. Designed by Lieutenant-Colonel Jonathan Williams of the United States Corps of Engineers, the fort was built from 1807 to 1811. It was one of the most modern coastal fortifications anywhere at that time and it was named after its builder in 1810. This engraving shows it as seen from The Battery, in its original setting. (Library of Congress, Washington, DC)

Academy as well a commander of the Corps of Engineers, he further took on the mantle of transforming theory into practice to provide protection to the largest city in the United States, which then had a population of about 100,000.

Such a formidable undertaking had not been seen since the 1760s, when the Spanish massively rebuilt and expanded the fortifications of Havana, Cuba, and San Juan, Puerto Rico. After decades of construction, these cities had been made next to impregnable, but with two cost factors that were contentious in a business community: firstly the amounts of money spent – from taxes that might have been lower or better spent elsewhere – had been enormous and, secondly, the space required to accommodate these works – some 11 hectares for San Juan – was huge. Thanks to Montalembert's ideas however, the bill would be much lower than in Havana or San Juan and the space required far smaller than what had been required to built Fort Jay/Columbus. Thus, Williams was something of a hero with the city's business community as well as with the New York state government. It was the standard procedure to submit fortification plans to the state governments, and Governor Daniel Tompkins was obviously pleased.

Even before his prototype fort was completed in 1811, which then made it the most formidable defense work ever constructed on the American coast, Williams was already planning several more casemated forts to protect the city. Construction started in 1807 on the North Battery, which was situated on a small island in the Hudson River about 200ft (60m) off Manhattan Island at the end of Hubert Street. It had 16 guns and was known as the Red Fort because of the red limestone used for its walls. Work continued in 1808 and 1809 on two smaller single-tiered circular casemate forts that would become known as Fort Gansevoort and Castle Clinton, originally known as the West Battery. The smaller size of these forts reflected the federal government's wish to control costs; the defenses of other harbors also had to be paid for. As they were, such forts could be built up later on if need be while nevertheless providing a redoubtable deterrent to any ship. Fort Gansevoort was at the water's edge on lower Manhattan at the end of Gansevoort Street and was also called the White Fort because its exterior masonry walls were whitewashed. It was armed with 16 guns and eventually demolished later in the 19th century. Castle Clinton was known as the West Battery before 1817, and it was situated on a small rocky island linked by a causeway with a drawbridge to Battery Park. It was armed with 28 guns and, during the War of 1812, was also the headquarters for the military command of New York City's defenses. The US Army left this fort in 1821 and it became an amusement park and concert hall, an immigration station that processed some eight million emigrants between 1855 and 1890, then housed the city aquarium until 1941, and is now a National Park Service monument in Battery Park. Its impressive walls are now part of the mainland owing

The West Battery in New York City, c.1815. Built on the western side of Battery Park on the tip New York's Lower Manhattan Island between 1808 and 1811, it was one of the redoubtable fortifications that protected the harbor of New York City. It was designed by Lt. Col. Williams and architect John McComb, Jr. Castle Williams can be seen farther east on Governors Island in the background. Renamed Castle Clinton in 1815, it was demilitarized in 1821. (Contemporary engraving; Library of Congress, Washington, DC)

Fort Wood serves as the base of the famous Statue of Liberty at the entrance of New York City's harbor. It was completed in 1811. It features a 12-pointed star layout and was meant as a 30-gun battery on the west side of the harbor's entrance to provide crossfire with other forts farther east. It was named Fort Wood after the War of 1812. It is situated on Bedoes Island, renamed Liberty Island since 1956. (Photograph taken in 1978 by Jack Boucher; Library of Congress, Washington, DC)

to landfilling. Work went on with smaller works to secure the harbor in the following years. Fort Gipson, named Crown Battery before 1812, was a circular fort of 14 guns built from 1809 on Oyster Island (later Ellis Island) and later demolished (the present battery was built in 1897).

One of the most famous sites in the world since the late 19th century had its foundations built as part of the defenses of New York harbor as they were planned by Williams. In 1810–11 the site of the small battery on Bedoes Island was totally eclipsed by a larger star fort having some 12 points, which constituted an ideal design for barbette batteries. It was armed with 30 cannon and named Fort Wood in 1814. From its site nearer to the New Jersey shore of the Hudson River, it was meant to interact with the other forts farther east. It was eventually decommissioned, and from 1886 the Statue of Liberty was placed in the center of the fort, where it stands today.

Many more forts were built in the New York City area to complement the powerful ones built during the Second System construction program, which had arguably transformed the city from a nearly defenseless metropolis

A   CASTLE WILLIAMS, NEW YORK CITY

This was a radical design of fort when it was built from 1807 to protect New York City's harbor. It was designed by Lt. Col. Jonathan Williams, commander of the United States Corps of Engineers, first superintendent of the West Point Military Academy, and a keen student of new theories of fortification from the time he spent in Paris assisting his great-uncle, United States ambassador Benjamin Franklin, from 1776 to 1785. Castle Williams was the prototype of a new era of coastal fortifications in the United States. It consisted of a large circular tower-like structure with 8ft-thick (2.4m) walls containing three tiers of casemates **(1)** armed with many cannon. Each level had

13 casemates that could hold 26 cannon, and there were also gun positions on its bomb-proof roof **(2)**. It rose to 40ft (12.2m) high and its diameter was 210ft (64m). Its wall was made of red sandstone and, initially was armed with 80 guns. This made it the strongest coastal defensive work constructed up to that time. It was finished in late 1810 or early 1811, and the name of "Castle Williams" was officially authorized to honor its designer's long and distinguished career. Its construction was followed by several smaller circular casemate forts, which made New York City go from being a practically undefended harbor to one of the most formidably lethal places anywhere for a hostile fleet to attack.

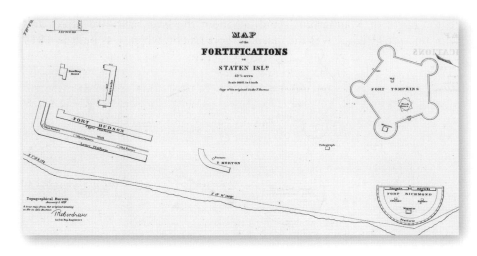

Fort Tompkins and Fort Richmond with the Fort Hudson and Fort Morton batteries on Staten Island. These forts were built from 1807 to cover the entrance to the Hudson River at the Narrows some 12 miles (19.3km) south of New York City. This 1827 plan shows the original layout before these forts were transformed in the 1840s and 1850s. (Library of Congress, Washington, DC)

to one of the most redoubtable areas for a naval force to attack. Construction started in 1807 on what would become Fort Tompkins, the first of several forts built on Staten Island to secure the Narrows – the entrance from the Atlantic into the Hudson River, 12 miles (19.3km) south of New York harbor. It also had two nearby outer batteries, Fort Morton and Fort Hudson, to the south. By 1812, this masonry pentagonal fort with its large round towers as bastions could be seen on top of a steep cliff, at the bottom of which also stood the semicircular Water Battery (later Fort Richmond) at the water's edge. Right across from this battery was Fort Diamond (renamed Lafayette in 1825) on Hendrick's Reef, a battery eventually armed with 72 cannon, begun in 1812 just off the Long Island shore of the river. On Denyse's Heights above Fort Diamond, Fort Lewis was built in 1814, which featured a blockhouse and emplacements for 30 guns. There were also the Bath Bay, Utrecht Bay, and Decatur blockhouses farther south on Long Island and facing the Atlantic. Farther northeast on Long Island was the sizeable town of Brooklyn, which faced Governors Island and New York City across the East River. During the War of 1812, forts Fireman, Lawrence, Greene, Cummings, and Masonic – the latter thanks to the Masonic Fraternity – were built to protect the town in case of an attack by an enemy force landing farther to the southeast.

In early August 1814, New York City was rife with rumors. It was said that the British fleet would come up to New York from Chesapeake Bay while a British army would come down from Montréal and attack the city. Residents, especially businessmen, had been concerned about the war for a while, but this time the threat seemed serious. On August 10, a meeting of all leading residents was held to organize the defense of the city and build more fortifications; men volunteered by their crafts, and much business and trade was suspended while forts and batteries were built at Brooklyn and Manhattan. News of the capture of Washington, DC, reached New York City on August 24 and its residents called for more troops. New York Governor Daniel Tompkins mobilized many more militiamen and, by the fall, some 20,000 New York State troops were on duty in New York City, which was transformed into a large armed camp. Every able-bodied man contributed either his services or his money to the city's defense, much of which was devoted to fortifications. Four blockhouses (one of which was named Fort Clinton) were built from August 1814 to guard the roads into the city from the north. They were located above Harlem on Manhattan Island. Guarding access to the north of Manhattan Island, at about the level of 123rd Street and Morningside Heights, was the masonry Fort Laight, which was built in 1814 like a square tower, and No. 4 Blockhouse. Then came Fort Clinton, also built in 1814 as a square stone structure, which may also have been No. 1 Blockhouse at the present Central Park level, possibly near 7th Avenue and 114th Street. No. 2 Blockhouse was at Morningside Avenue and 114th Street and No. 3 Blockhouse at Morningside Avenue and 121st Street. Farther east facing the East River was Fort Stevens, built in 1814, which included a blockhouse as well as several guns. Fort Horn was at the head of Morningside Park, named after New York Militia Major Joseph Horn, who supervised the building of fortifications at McGowan's Pass. At last, on February 11, 1815, the British sloop HMS *Favorite* brought the official news to New York City that the war was over and there was much rejoicing over the prospect of the resumption of trade and industry in that great business-minded city.

Middle states

The most important cities to protect in the middle states were Philadelphia, Pennsylvania, and Baltimore, Maryland, each with a population of about 55,000 souls. Washington, the new federal capital since 1800 in the equally new District of Columbia, had only about 9,000 inhabitants. The federal bureaucracy was then quite small and some of its employees were still working in Philadelphia, the previous capital.

Philadelphia was reached after a fairly long navigation by the Delaware River, but before reaching the city, ships had to pass within the range of Fort Mifflin's guns on Mud Island, at the confluence of the Delaware and Schuylkill rivers. The fort had been built from 1771, taken and retaken during the American Revolution and somewhat abandoned after the war. Possibly its most remarkable feature was the tooth-saw shaped bastions that formed the

Fort Mifflin was rebuilt between 1798 and 1803 in order to protect Philadelphia. It was on the site and essentially retained the layout of an earlier fort built on Mud Island at the confluence of the Delaware and Schuylkill rivers. It had a peculiar plan featuring elements of both the star and bastion designs. Its south curtain wall, facing the Delaware River, was especially notable for its tooth-saw bastions, which held most of the artillery. (Photograph taken in 1971 by Jack Boucher; Library of Congress, Washington, DC)

Plan of Fort Norfolk, Norfolk, Virginia, *c*.1810. Authorized to be built in 1794 as one of the 19 forts to protect American harbors, most of Fort Norfolk was constructed in 1810. It featured a large and powerful semi-circular battery covering the entrance of the Elizabeth River as well as bastions, a ravelin, and glacis on the landward side. It did not see action during the War of 1812, possibly because of its strength considering the high level of British naval activity in the area. The fort's garrison was removed during the 1820s as a result of Fort Monroe being built, but it was later reactivated and has remained an army base ever since. (Library of Congress, Washington, DC)

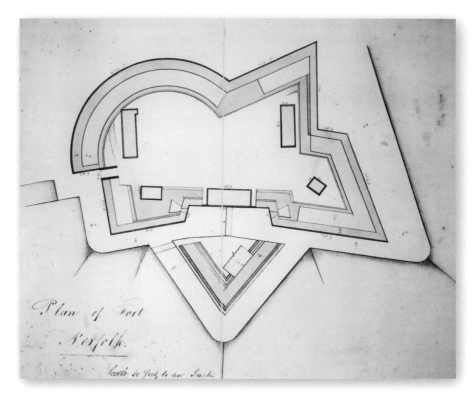

The Guard House at Fort McHenry, Baltimore, in 1814 and 1829. The fort's building at the time of the 1814 British attack had one story with an attic and featured sloped roofs. As this interpretative illustration shows, in 1829 the buildings were remodeled, raised with a second story, and provided with elegant verandahs. (Fort McHenry National Monument, National Park Service, Baltimore)

curtain wall on the river's edge and which had most of the fort's 29 guns. In 1794 it was one of the very few derelict forts that was considered repairable for incorporation into the First System, a task performed until 1798 by Pierre L'Enfant, the French engineer chiefly remembered for his remarkable urban plan of Washington, DC. Various reconstructions and new features such as casemates were further added by Lieutenant-Colonel Rochefontaine. Fort Gaines, a small and temporary six-gun battery, was built in 1814 about 400yds (365m) northeast of Fort Mifflin on the Delaware River. Farther south, a few small batteries were built by militiamen in the area of Wilmington,

Delaware, which otherwise had no major fortifications. Fortunately, the British did not raid that area.

Insofar as raids were concerned, the Chesapeake Bay presented better and safer opportunities than the Delaware. Its mouth on the Atlantic was wide so that ships could pass outside of the effective range of shore batteries and be quite safe once they reached Chesapeake Bay. They then had the choice to raid communities in the bay area, follow the river until Baltimore was in view to the north, or take the Potomac River west to reach Washington, DC. The geography of the Chesapeake and the very large area to protect was beyond the possibilities of the First and Second systems of fortifications, as well as, to some extent, the technological possibilities of artillery ranges at that time. Since there was nothing afloat and not much on shore to stop large British warships, the temptation to mount raids in the area was considerable and might even bring in sizeable amounts of prize money.

Norfolk, Virginia, was the only locality at the bay's entrance that had a fort with a regular-army garrison. A First System work had been built there

Francis Scott Key watching the bombardment of Fort McHenry by the dawn's early light of September 13, 1814. A lawyer, he was part of a delegation negotiating the release of American prisoners and was compelled to remain on board a Royal Navy warship. The night's intense bombardment inspired his poem "The Star-Spangled Banner," which became the words of the United States' national anthem. (Print after Thomas Moran; Library of Congress, Washington, DC)

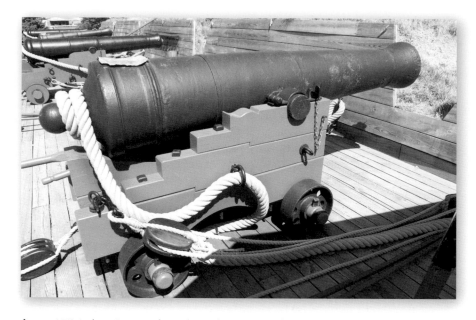

A French 36-pdr naval cannon mounted in one of the shore batteries in front of Fort McHenry, 1814. In 1813, the French consulate in Baltimore transferred 56 guns, half of them 36-pdrs, to the United States, and many were installed in the city's fortifications. The large 36-pdrs were especially valuable in coastal forts. Such a cannon weighed 5 tons, required 12 pounds of powder to fire a shot every two minutes at an effective range of 1½ miles and needed a crew of 21 men. They were installed in the Water Battery on the shoreline in front of the fort. (Fort McHenry National Monument, National Park Service, Baltimore)

from 1794, but it was found inadequate and was torn down and replaced by a Second System fort in 1808. It had 29 guns, including 27 heavy 24-pdrs that faced the bay, mounted mostly in a semi-circular barbette battery. The fort also featured bastions and a ravelin. Nearby, across the Norfolk River's entrance, was Fort Nelson, an irregular bastioned work of the First System that was armed with 33 cannon in 1813. These forts of Norfolk's second line of defense were never attacked, but the unfinished fortifications on Craney Island farther north facing Hampton Roads, which formed its first line, repulsed a sizeable British landing attempt by some 1,500 men on April 22, 1813. There was just a blockhouse with a few guns, unfinished earthworks, and a small battery of six cannon some distance to the north. These few cannon were served expertly by the American gunners and forced the British longboats to head out after suffering some losses. These included some men of the renegade Independent Companies of Foreigners made up of French prisoners of war. Their comrades later exacted their revenge by murdering, raping, and robbing the citizens of nearby Hampton as they likely had previously on hapless Portuguese and Spaniards. This undisciplined unit, which served American propaganda wonderfully, was shipped back and eventually disbanded; by then, nearly all Americans knew about the atrocities they had committed. Britain and the United States were then probably the world's only countries that had a free press.

In August 1814 the British were back in force. On August 19–20 some 4,000 troops were landed south of Washington, DC. It was not a fortified city and did not have any sizeable defense works until Fort Warbuton, renamed Fort Washington, was inaugurated in 1809. It was situated south of Alexandria, Virginia, on a site overlooking the Potomac River, which George Washington had identified as suitable for such a fort. It consisted of star-shaped earthwork, in front of which was a circular battery with 13 guns. The British troops did not approach the fort, but instead marched northwards inland, met and beat an American army at Bladensburg, Maryland, and then entered the defenseless capital on August 24. As is well known, the public buildings were burned, including the White House. What is not well known is that this action was in retaliation for the Americans' wanton destruction of the public buildings of York (Toronto), the capital of Upper Canada, in April 1813. This sort of regrettable behavior had rather upset many Canadians and Britons. Meanwhile, British ships were moving up the Potomac River and came to Fort Washington on August 27. Shortly after the British fleet started bombarding it, its commander ordered the fort blown up and its cannon spiked. Thus, the British fleet sailed on unopposed. So far, the Chesapeake Bay defenses they had encountered were negligible and American defenders were apparently crumbling; the citizens of Alexandria, Virginia, had even paid a hefty ransom in order to escape pillage.

The British now sailed towards Baltimore. On the way, they passed the town of Annapolis, Maryland, which had Fort Severn, a circular masonry structure built in 1808 bearing 11 guns. It was not regularly garrisoned except during the summer of 1814, but the British did not attack. Fort Madison, a small semi-elliptical work armed with 13 guns, was also built in 1808 on nearby Carr Point and, half a mile (800m) to the north, the most curiously named Fort Nonsense, which consisted of a circular earthwork of 80ft (24m) in diameter.

On September 12, Baltimore was in view of the 50 British warships. To defend the city, some 14,000 militiamen joined 1,000 regulars. The most important fortification in the area was Fort McHenry, which guarded the access to the city's port. It was a large First System earth-and-masonry fort built from 1799 to 1805 on the plans of French engineer Jean Fontin. It was a pentagon with five bastions, which gave it the shape of a five-pointed star, and was armed with some 30 guns, in addition to three water batteries. More features were added later on, notably a water battery in 1814 that had heavy French naval guns including some 36-pdrs. A boom consisting of ships' masts fastened together was laid to block the 600yd-wide (549m) harbor entrance between the fort and Lazaretto Point.

Just past midnight on September 13, British bomb ketches and rocket ships started an intense bombardment of Fort McHenry that lasted 25 hours. Some 1,800 explosive

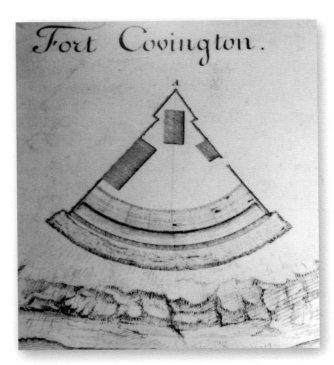

Plan of Fort Covington, Baltimore. This fort was a semi-circular battery situated 1½ miles (2.4km) due west of Fort McHenry. In 1814 it was armed with seven 24-pdrs and, together with the nearby Babcock battery armed with six 18-pdrs, it guarded access toward Ridgelys Cove, which was south of Baltimore and otherwise unprotected by fortifications. Fort Covington's guns opened fire together with Fort McHenry's guns during the British attack on Baltimore in September 1814. (Detail from an 1819 plan by Captain William Tell Poussin, United States Corps of Engineers; United States National Archives, Washington, DC)

B NEXT PAGE: FORT MCHENRY, BALTIMORE

Of all the forts of the War of 1812, Fort McHenry in Baltimore is undoubtedly the most famous and, for Americans, the most beloved fort in the history of the United States of America. This is due to the valiant defense put up by its garrison in September 1814, when a large British fleet came up Chesapeake Bay and bombarded Fort McHenry for 25 hours. As all Americans know, the British bombardment inspired patriotism and resolve, which was stirringly put into words by lawyer Francis Scott Key who witnessed the event in his poem "The Star-Spangled Banner." It immediately became very popular, was put to music, and is now the national anthem of the United States.

The fort itself was a First System work to protect access to Baltimore's harbor, which it certainly did brilliantly in September 1814. Construction began in 1799 and was completed by 1805. Its curtain walls were of earth and masonry. Engineer Jean Fontin's design was not revolutionary, but resulted in a fortification that could resist an attack by land as well as by sea. The fort was laid out on a pentagon plan with five bastions (1), one at each corner, which gave it its "star" shape, and the main gate was protected by a ravelin (2). There was a ditch outside its walls. Each bastion had four guns mounted en barbette with up to another 30 installed in three shore batteries (3) in front of the fort, facing the water.

bombs were fired at the fort, which some expected to be destroyed, but it stood up to the bombardment well. The great majority of the fort's guns could not reach the British ships, which stayed safely outside their range of 1½ miles (2.4km). As a result, most of the British bombs and rockets fell short and missed the fort. The bombardment's noise was deafening and could be heard by the worried population as far as 48 miles (77km) away. Meanwhile, a British landing had been repulsed by American militiamen at North Point, and another west of Fort McHenry had been foiled by its guns and those of the Fort Covington battery. It became obvious to the British that Baltimore's defenses were much stronger than expected. The bombardment ceased at 1.00am on September 14, and later in the morning the British fleet sailed away. The Americans were elated; their coastal defense had stood up against a major attack and the confident fort commander, Corps of Artillery Major George Armistead, wanted an even larger flag for his fort in order to defy the British.

The South

Coastal fortifications were not as numerous in the mostly rural and more sparsely populated southern states. At the outset of the War of 1812 there were no federal garrisons in North Carolina, only Fort Johnson armed with 12 guns at the Cape Fear River below Wilmington, and a battery of five cannon near Beaufort. In South Carolina, Charleston had a company of artillery to serve the main forts that guarded the harbor: Fort Mechanic (also called Fort Darrell), an enclosed work that featured a masonry battery at White Point Garden in the town's center; Fort Johnson, a brick-and-wood

Fort Mims, 1813. Situated in present-day Alabama, this large settlers' fort was the scene of one of the most horrible massacres in American history. On August 30, 1813, as many as 520 men, women, and children were killed by Creek warriors when they captured the fort. Initially built on a square plan, it had up to 17 buildings within, including a blockhouse (at upper right) and some of the palisade was being doubled (at left) for added security. The fort was destroyed after its capture. (Detail from the contemporary map of Fort Mims and Environs by Ferdinand Leigh Claiborne; Alabama Department of Archives and History, Montgomery)

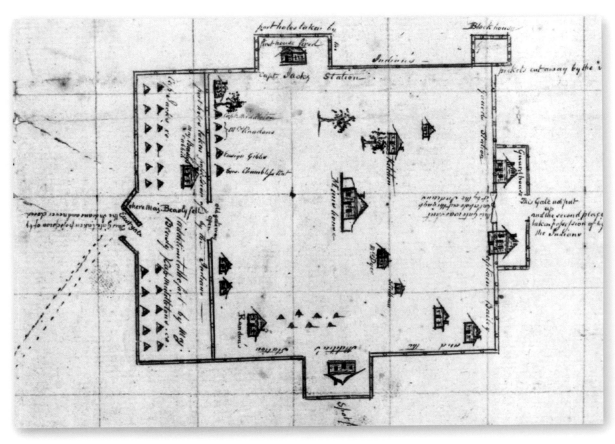

quadrilateral work with 26 guns built in 1809 on James Island; Fort Moultrie on Sullivan's Island, which was originally of wood but was rebuilt with brick in 1809; and Fort Pinckney, a two-tier casemated masonry fort armed with 30 guns built in 1809–10 over a previous fort on Shutes Folly Island.

Fort Hawkins (or Fort Benjamin Hawkins) was built in 1806 at Macon, Georgia, on the western frontier of the state, and was garrisoned with light dragoons in 1811–12. It was a large stockade fort with blockhouses, and was meant to keep an eye on the sometime hostile Indians and to serve as a staging area for General Andrew Jackson's forces against the Creeks. Much farther into the wilderness, about 45 miles (72km) north of Mobile, Alabama, was Fort Mims, an American settler's stockade enclosure where, in the summer of 1813, some 550 people sought refuge from hostile Creek warriors. But the Creeks took the fort on August 30, 1813, and killed or captured nearly all within except for 36 who managed to escape. An outraged American force of about 2,500 men under General Andrew Jackson later cleared the Creeks from Alabama, killing at least 850 at the battle of Horseshoe Bend on March 27, 1814.

A new work at Point Petre on the St Mary's River had 200 soldiers. On the coast at Five Fathom Hole, 3 miles below Savannah, was an eight-gun masonry battery, but with no regular garrison. In June 1813 the city of Savannah, which had about 7,000 inhabitants, was considered by Secretary of War John Armstrong to be "more exposed than any other" because "few expenses of public money have been made," and he proposed to protect it by a "chain of redans on three of its sides," with redoubts on the fourth side, which was most vulnerable.

Louisiana had an entirely different background, having been originally French and then Spanish since the 1760s, and then French again briefly in 1803, when it was sold by Napoleon to the United States that same year. New Orleans was by far the largest city on the Gulf Coast, with some 18,000 citizens. Its access at the mouth of the Mississippi River was guarded by several small forts and batteries, but no formidable fortifications had been put up by the French or Spanish. The Americans initially retained only Fort St Philip and Fort St Charles, which housed regular-army gunners, and the Bayou St John battery below New Orleans. All were improved and expanded. In the case of Fort St Philip at the Plaquemines Bend, it was reconstructed from 1808 into a redoubtable enclosed twin battery that could hold 24 guns and was considered the only really effective work guarding the lower Mississippi. A battery was ordered built at English Turn the following year. While these forts provided some protection from the south, there was no defense against an enemy force landing on the shores of Lake Borgne, which was only some 20 miles (32km) east of New Orleans, although there was some question as to whether that part of West Florida still belonged to Spain.

After Major-General James Wilkinson solved the issue by the United States' military occupation of the area up to Mobile, Alabama, in April 1813, the Americans built Fort Bowyer on Mobile Point, an earth-and-wood enclosed work armed with about 14 guns, built on a semi-circular plan facing the sea with curtain walls and a bastion facing landward. It repulsed a British attack on September 14–16, 1814. Nevertheless, the east flank through Lake Borgne remained basically undefended. The British noticed this and, in late December, landed a large army there. Field fortifications were put up

at Chalmette, where, on January 8, 1815, General Andrew Jackson and his mixed force of American militiamen and regulars inflicted a stunning defeat on the British troops that tried to storm these defenses by a frontal assault. The dejected British went back to their ships and, on February 7, besieged Fort Bowyer, which now had 22 guns and 385 men. After a brave resistance against overwhelming odds, the American garrison surrendered on February 12 when the fort became too vulnerable from British batteries on the landward side. The British were planning to attack Mobile when, two days later, word arrived that peace had been concluded at Ghent on December 24, 1814. The short-lived but glorious Fort Bowyer was totally reconstructed as the much larger Fort Morgan.

Fort Osage, Missouri, built in 1808. It had an elongated pentagon plan with four large blockhouses and buildings that formed a V-shaped curtain wall. It held a small regular garrison and officials of the Indian Agency. It was abandoned in 1813 and reoccupied from 1815 to 1827. (Photograph by John Stanton, Wikimedia)

Western and northern frontier forts

The designs, technology, and materials used to build inland forts on the western frontier, and often far in the wilderness, were much cruder than for coastal forts. The latest trends in fortress layouts were not necessary in a

---

C FORT LERNOULT/DETROIT, AUGUST 1812

Founded by the French as a fortified post in 1701, the city of Detroit evolved as a small "metropolis of the Great Lakes" thanks to its strategic location on the banks of the Detroit River, which linked lakes Erie and Huron. On the bluff overlooking Detroit was Fort Lernout, named after British Captain Richard B. Lernoult, who had this work built in 1778–79. It consisted of an earth-and-wood four-pointed star layout with the buildings within aligned in a cross pattern. The artillery was mounted on individual wooden galleries. The Stars and Stripes rose on the fort on July 11, 1796, when the Americans took possession of Detroit and Michigan following Jay's Treaty. The fort was usually referred to as Fort Detroit thereafter.

The fort had not changed much by June 1812 except that, according to a Canadian plan made in January that year, the inside buildings were now rebuilt in line with the curtain walls, providing a square parade ground at its center. In June and July, Detroit was the assembly point of an American invading army under the command of General William Hull, who was also governor of Michigan. The rather amateurish invaders did not get very far and were back in Detroit by early August when a mixed force of British regulars, Canadian militiamen,

and Indian warriors led by General Isaac Brock and Chief Tecumseh showed up outside the city and blockaded it. The besieging force of about 1,300 men (including 330 regulars and 400 Canadians) was actually much smaller than the 2,200 defenders (including 600 regulars of the 4th United States Infantry), but Brock had his militiamen march around wearing surplus coats of the 41st British Regiment while Tecumseh's warriors appeared everywhere making loud war whoops. On August 16, gunners of the Canadian Provincial Marine started bombarding the fort. A rather panicked (and rumored drunk) Gen. Hull, believing that he was being set upon by many thousands of enemies and fearing a massacre by Indians, surrendered – against the advice of most of his officers – apparently after a shell landed rather too close for comfort in the fort. Detroit remained under the Union Jack until September 1813, when it was evacuated by the British and Canadian forces following Commodore Oliver Perry's victory on Lake Erie. The fort was renamed Fort Shelby after Governor Isaac Shelby of Kentucky. It was turned over to the city of Detroit in 1826 and razed the following year. Its site is at the corner of Fort and Shelby streets.

context that was unlikely to involve heavy artillery and bombardments from bomb ketches. Settlers in these areas built hundreds of forts and blockhouses as protection against the ever-present threat of Indian attacks. Those forts built in the 1790s by the nascent US Army tended to be more elaborate versions of the same type of design, which usually consisted of a square or rectangular layout with barracks two stories high acting as walls, with elaborate blockhouses as bastions at each corner, sometimes featuring a *guérite* (watchtower) on the top. A triangular stockade ravelin with another blockhouse at its point might also extend from one side.

In 1803 much thought was given to the design of frontier forts and, in March, Colonel Henry Burbeck, commander of the Corps of Artillery and formerly chief engineer when the corps included engineering, came up with a design for "most easily constructed and sufficiently defensible" posts "in an Indian Country," drawing on his 1790s campaign experiences. This was a simple square layout, suggested to be 120ft² (36.5m²) with two blockhouses on opposite corners to be two stories high and 20ft² (6m²) "so placed as to afford a Flank fire from every part of the Post, which with a fire from the other buildings would effectually annoy any number of Indians which might attempt an assault." The buildings within acted partly as walls, their timber "slightly hewed and the spaces between plastered with clay or lime." The magazine was recommended to be "in the form of a cone, without any wood except for the door." An outer stockade laid out in a three-quarters circle around each blockhouse completed the exterior obstacles.

That this was not followed to the letter is obvious, but it was a guide. Forts actually came in all shapes and sizes. Relatively few of them had garrisons of regular troops before the War of 1812. In the Mississippi, Missouri, and Ohio Valley are as taken in their broadest sense, only Fort Massac, Illinois; Fort Hampton, Tennessee; Fort Belle Fontaine (north of St Louis, Missouri); Fort Osage (near Sibley, Missouri); Fort Madison, Iowa; Fort Knox (Vincennes); and Fort Wayne, Indiana, had detachments of US Army soldiers. Of these, Fort Madison, built in 1808, was attacked by the Indians in April 1809 and in March and September 1812, and was besieged from July to September 1814, during which its small garrison

Fort Madison, Iowa, *c.*1810. This fort, built in 1808, was attacked four times by Indians between 1809 and 1814, when it was abandoned. It had two of its blockhouses (1 and 2) placed at each end of one wall (bottom), its stockade coming to a point and then extending in a type of spur, at the end of which was another blockhouse. The outside "Factory" was a trading store. (Plan by Bill Whittaker, Wikimedia)

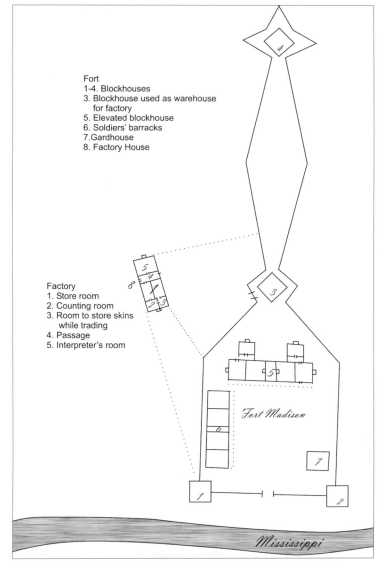

Fort
1–4. Blockhouses
3. Blockhouse used as warehouse for factory
5. Elevated blockhouse
6. Soldiers' barracks
7. Gardhouse
8. Factory House

Factory
1. Store room
2. Counting room
3. Room to store skins while trading
4. Passage
5. Interpreter's room

Fort Madison

Mississippi

managed to slip away, abandoning the fort. Back in the summer of 1811, US Army regulars and militia moved against the Indians in Indiana under the command of Gen. William Henry Harrison. In October they built Fort Harrison (Terre Haute, Indiana), which was square with two-story blockhouses at opposite ends, and, on November 7, they defeated an Indian force at Tippecanoe (near Lafayette, Indiana). Following the declaration of war in 1812, Fort Harrison was attacked and partly destroyed by the Indians, but not taken. Farther north however, Fort Dearborn (Chicago, Illinois) was built in 1803 with two blockhouses at each end. One wall was destroyed and most of its garrison and dependents were slaughtered by Potawatomi Indians in August 1812.

The most northerly post was Fort Mackinac, Michigan, often called Michilimackinac, built in 1780 by the British and transferred to the United States in 1796. It was situated on Mackinac Island, within sight of the magnificent Mackinac Strait that connects lakes Huron and Michigan. Not very far to the north was the British Fort St Joseph, on the island of the same name, which had the most westerly garrison of regular redcoats in Canada. Its commander, Captain Charles Roberts, learned earlier than his American counterpart, artillery Lieutenant Porter Hanks, that war had been declared. He then mustered a force of Royal Veterans – a unit of aged soldiers known for its love of rum, but whose men were often battle-tested – and Canadian fur traders. They all appeared before Fort Mackinac on July 17, 1812. After manhandling a small canon up a cliff near the fort, which was fired a few times, the American fort surrendered and its garrison learned that the United States had declared war. This was the earliest of many engagements of the War of 1812. Fort Mackinac made a much better base than Fort St Joseph, and the British and Canadians moved there. From there, the British, Canadians, and their Indian allies soon ruled over the western Great Lakes. There were various forays and, on July 20, 1814, FortShelby at Prairie du Chien, Wisconsin, a stockade fort with two blockhouses, was taken by its opponents only two months after it had been built. On August 4, 1814, the Americans tried to retake Fort Mackinac, but were repulsed.

Fort Mackinac on Mackinac Island, Michigan. Built by the British in 1780, it was turned over to the United States in 1796 and was captured in July 1812 by a mixed British and Canadian force. The Americans failed to retake it in August 1814. It was returned to the United States after the war. It was (and remains) sited on a cliff overlooking a small landing and still has its irregular triangular plan with blockhouses. The base of the walls and the first story of the blockhouses are made of stone. Some other structures within the fort postdate the War of 1812. (Author's collection)

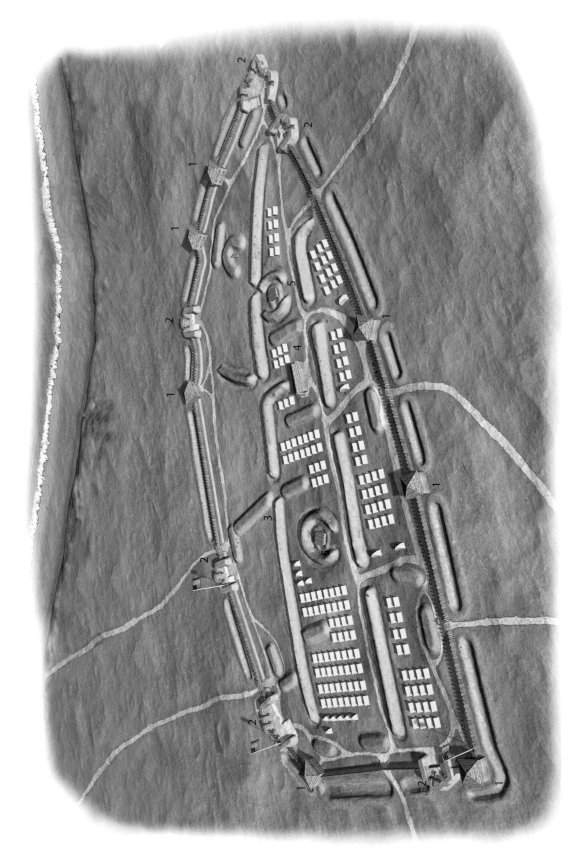

32

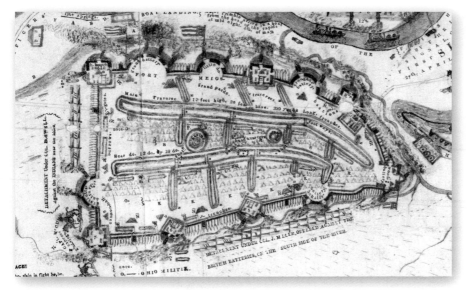

Plan of Fort Meigs, Ohio, during its sieges from April 27 to May 9 and July 21–28, 1813. Built from February 1, 1813, by Gen. William Henry Harrison's army on the southern shore of the Maumee River (now Perrysburg, Ohio), the fort consisted of a large 8-acre (32,000m²) area surrounded by a 15ft-high stockade punctuated by seven large blockhouses and five semi-circular batteries according this plan. Within the fort were trench-like "traverses" that gave additional protection from bombardment. In the event, both British sieges failed. (Detail from the "Plan of Fort Meigs… by an officer on the Kentucky Militia," by William Sebree; Library of Congress, Washington, DC)

Farther east, on the United States shore of the Detroit and St Clair rivers that linked lakes Erie and Huron, stood the town of Detroit. Its 1,000 inhabitants made it the metropolis of the central Great Lakes. Founded by the French in 1701, Detroit had been British from 1760 to 1796 and American thereafter. By 1811 the town's stockade had mostly been removed, although a few small batteries were built near the river. On July 12, 1812, it was the base from which General William Hull crossed the Detroit River with US Army regulars and militiamen and invaded the sparsely settled western Upper Canada. But they soon sought refuge back in Detroit when General Sir Isaac Brock approached with a mixed force of 330 British and 400 Canadian troops with 600 Indian warriors led by Chief Tecumseh. Huddled in Fort Lernoult (also called Detroit), a four-point earth-and-wood structure with up to 24 guns, Hull had some 600 regulars and about 1,600 militiamen, mostly from Ohio. Convinced that he faced a much stronger force and fearing Indian outrages, he surrendered on August 16 after a short bombardment from the five British field guns. The British held Detroit until they were compelled to evacuate it and western Upper Canada following the American naval victory on Lake Erie on September 10, 1813, and the battle of the Thames, where Tecumseh was killed on October 5.

D FORT MEIGS, OHIO, 1813

The construction of Fort Meigs by Gen. William Henry Harrison's army started in February 1813. Built on a wide bluff near the Maumee River, it was originally meant to be a large temporary base and a supply depot for an intended invasion of western Canada. It was therefore much bigger than the average frontier fort, but did not have barracks because troops assembling there were not expected to remain for very long. Its architecture was typical of western forts in that it had a stockade with sturdy timber blockhouses (1) two stories high and about 32ft (9.7m) wide at various intervals along it. Less typical was its huge size and its earthworks. There were six semi-circular batteries (2) built along the curtain walls, each armed with two to four 18-pdr cannon. The platforms were 5ft (1.5m) high, the parapets 8ft (2.4m) tall, and the embrasures 2½ft (0.76m) wide. The stockade's logs were 15ft (4.5m) high with 3ft embedded in the ground, and

were protected by an 8ft-high (2.4m) embankment. Inside the fort were 12ft-high (3.6m) and very long traverses (earthen mounds) (3), which crossed the fort from end to end and were intended to protect the tent city within from enemy artillery fire. Except for a quartermaster's storehouse (4) and two powder magazines (5), there were no other permanent buildings within the fort. The powder magazines were nearly square at about 15ft (4.5m) to a side and were mostly built below ground level.

Instead of serving as a United States invasion base, Fort Meigs became instead a pivotal defense point. It proved to be an effective and resilient work. When the British, Canadians, and Indians moved into northern Ohio in May 1813 and again in July 1813, the American garrison repulsed them at both sieges of Fort Meigs, thus preventing an invasion of the northwestern United States.

Fort Stephenson, Ohio, 1813. A: blockhouse; D: hospital; E: storehouses; F: commissary's storehouse; G: magazine; H: main gate; K: wicker gates; O: well. The numbers 4, 3, 2, and 1 represent respectively the glacis, the dry ditch, the embankment, and the line of pickets that made up the curtain wall. (Contemporary engraving; Private collection)

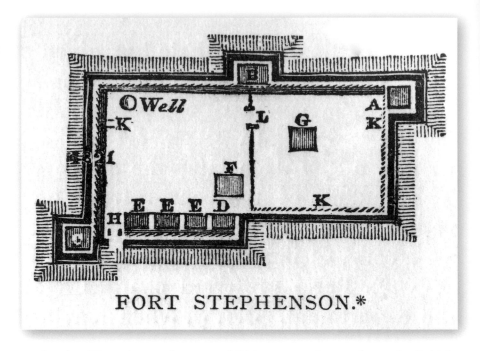

FORT STEPHENSON.*

South of Detroit was the state of Ohio, scene of many forays by British, Canadian, and Indian opponents. Fort Miami (Maumee, Ohio) was a bastioned earthwork surrounded by a ditch built by the British in 1794 and evacuated in 1796. In 1812, Gen. Harrison felt that it was too exposed and withdrew its American garrison, which was soon replaced by a British one, which held the fort until 1817.

Early in the War of 1812, the Americans lost major forts such as forts Mackinac and Lernoult, as well as suffering a major defeat at the River Raisin. By January 1813, only Fort Wayne, Indiana, remained. General Harrison, from February 2, established a base named Fort Meigs that was meant as a temporary supply depot and staging area for marching on Canada. It consisted of a large rectangular area whose earth-and-stockade walls were punctuated by batteries and blockhouses and it was soon filled with over 1,200 soldiers and militiamen. But it was the British, Canadians, and Indians who invaded northern Ohio and besieged Fort Meigs (Perrysburg, Ohio) from May 1–9. They were thwarted when United States reinforcements showed up, but they tried and failed again in July and moved against Fort Stephenson (Freemont, Ohio), which consisted of a rectangular stockade with three blockhouses built in 1812 near the Sandusky River. On July 30, 1813, a strong force under General Proctor and Tecumseh arrived in the area and fort commander Major George Croghan, 17th United States Infantry, opted to defend it with his

E FORT STEPHENSON, OHIO, 1813

This frontier fort was originally built in 1812 about 100yds (91.5m) northwest of the Sandusky River on a rising bluff. It had a prairie on its eastern side and a plain on the others. This gave it an unobstructed field of fire all around. The original fort was quite small, being on a square plan of about 100yds to each side of its stockade, which had two blockhouses on the northern side (1). It was enlarged sometime later, its size being doubled and

now having a rectangular plan with a blockhouse at its southwestern corner (2). It also had a ditch 6ft (1.8m) wide by 6ft (1.8m) deep, and was said to have old bayonets nailed to the top of its 18ft-high (5.4m) stockade logs.

The fort proved capable of repulsing an assault by British regulars on August 2, 1813, with its small-but-valiant garrison inflicting heavy casualties on the enemy.

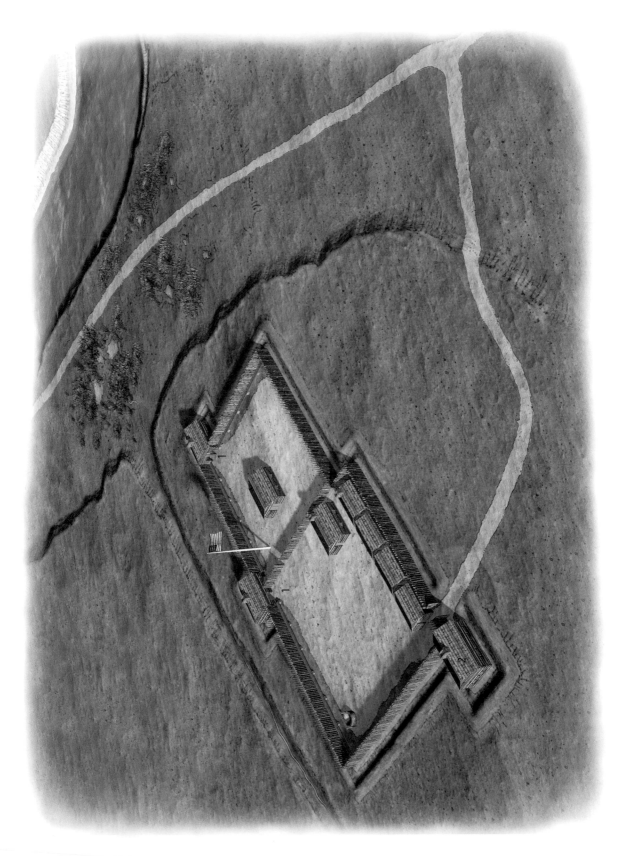

160 men and one field gun instead of destroying it and evacuating as instructed by Gen. Harrison. On August 2, some 360 men of the 41st Foot stormed the fort, but were repulsed, losing 96 casualties to the Americans' fire at the ravine near the north side's stockade, the garrison suffering only one killed and seven wounded. The Indians had offered "no assistance whatever" and the British force retreated to Canada.

Many stockade defenses were built to protect American communities throughout the Northwest. General George Sanderson's recollection of the fort built at Cleveland, Ohio, in 1813 is an example:

> Settlers in the vicinity of Sandusky and along the southwest shore of the lake [Lake Erie] had fallen victims to the atrocious mode of warfare adopted by [British General] Proctor and the uncivilized Indians who followed him. It was therefore natural that the inhabitants of Cleveland should feel some alarm… A stockade was erected at the foot of Ontario street, on the bank of the lake, made of pickets, reinforced in the interior with bags filled with sand, which made the place one of some strength, and though it would not have withstood the attack of a very large force, yet it answered the purpose in some measure, and produced a feeling of security. This was called Fort Huntington, in honor of our second Governor.

Clevelanders were luckier than most because the "stockade was provided with two pieces of artillery and garrisoned by regulars." Indeed, there were no major forts farther east along the southern shore of Lake Erie. Even at the important naval base of Erie, Pennsylvania, there were only two blockhouses built in 1813–14, the main one on Garrison Hill being called Fort Wayne. The 1794 stockade with four blockhouses at Fort Le Boeuf (Waterford, Pennsylvania) was used as a prison camp in 1813–14.

Amazingly, except for Fort Niagara, the Americans had no major fortifications along the northern borders of New York, Vermont, and Maine. As elsewhere, there were many batteries and stockades, a few of which saw action during the war. The small town of Buffalo, New York, had the earthwork Fort Tompkins, which was armed with seven guns with a few small auxiliary batteries, and the Black Rock blockhouse, all of which were

Fort Niagara, c.1810. This view taken from the Canadian shore shows that the main features of the fort were, on the whole, essentially the same as when the British captured it from the French in 1759. The British added two stone blockhouse-like redoubts, which came with the fort when it was turned over to the Americans in 1796. In 1812 the stone "French Castle" built in the 1720s was still the fort's largest building, and its roof was transformed into a gun-battery site shortly after the hostilities started for occasional artillery duels with nearby Fort George across the mouth of the Niagara River. However, in December 1813, the fort was captured by a British surprise night attack. The Americans did not try to retake it. (Private collection)

captured by the British forces in December 1813. Nearby Niagara Falls, New York, had Fort Schlosser, a square bastioned earthwork destroyed by the British in December 1813. A similar fate befell the small Fort Gray at Lewiston, New York.

Fort Niagara (Youngstown, New York) had been built from 1726 by the French to guard the strategically important western end of Lake Ontario at the mouth of the Niagara River. Impressive Vauban-style earthworks had been constructed across its peninsula from 1755, and in 1766 the British added two large stone redoubts within. US Army troops garrisoned the fort from 1796. Apart from various changes in service buildings, the gate shifting position sometime before 1810, and the roof of the stone "French Castle" being transformed into an elevated battery in late 1812, there were no major changes during the war. It was taken in a British surprise night assault on December 19, 1813, and flew the Union Jack until May 1815.

Farther east, Oswego, New York, which previously had some sizeable forts, had only a well-sited but decrepit earthwork. This was taken and destroyed by the British on May 6, 1814, after a valiant defense. The large United States naval base at Sackets Harbor had the 1812 Fort Tomkins, an earthwork fort mounting 20 guns with a blockhouse within. There were also several associated small batteries and earthwork lines with several redoubts, Fort Kentucky having 20 guns and Fort Virginia 16. Along the southern shore of the St Lawrence River was Ogdensburg, New York, which

Plan of the fortified cantonment at Plattsburgh, New York, September 1814. Barracks and other buildings are surrounded by a stockade with large octagonal blockades. The Saranac River and the town is at the right, and Plattsburgh Bay in Lake Champlain is below. (Library of Congress, Washington, DC)

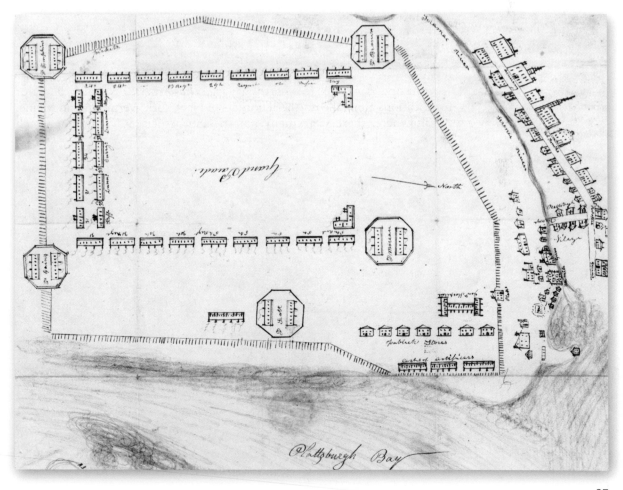

had only a small redan battery that was easily taken by British and Canadian troops on February 22, 1813. A stockade fort with four corner blockhouses was built by the US Army in 1813 at French Mills, New York, the locality's name being changed to Fort Covington. It was abandoned in February 1814 and burned by the British forces soon thereafter. Plattsburgh, New York, was the most important US Army staging area east of the Great Lakes during the war. The large irregular pentagon-shaped Cantonment Plattsburgh was built from 1812, a base with over 40 buildings surrounded by a stockade dotted with five large blockhouses at the confluence of the Saranac River and Lake Champlain. Farther up the river were a few redoubts built in 1814: Fort Brown (eight guns), Fort Moreau (12 guns), and Fort Scott (eight guns). Plattsburgh was brilliantly defended from September 6–11, 1814, by General Alexander Macomb and Commodore Thomas Macdonough against a large British attack. On the Vermont side of Lake Champlain, Burlington had 13 guns mounted behind earthworks at the present Battery Park, which exchanged fire with British gunboats in June 1813, as did Fort Cassin in 1814, the small earthwork armed with seven guns near Vergennes. There were no notable fortifications farther east, the northern borders of Vermont and Maine having a range of imposing wilderness mountains. It should be noted that these were the scene of large-scale smuggling, notably at Vermont's "Smuggler's Notch," and it has been calculated that Canada might even have run out of some food had it not been for this brisk illicit trade.

BRITISH NORTH AMERICA

At the time of the American declaration of hostilities, British North America's population of European origin numbered about 500,000, of which about 300,000 were descendants of the settlers of New France, the others being of those from the British Isles. The number of Indians was unknown, but perhaps

Eastern British North America. This was essentially the configuration of what became Canada at the time of the War of 1812. The area was divided into several colonies (or provinces). Lower Canada (now Québec) was the most extensively settled, with a population of about 300,000. Next came rapidly growing Upper Canada (now Ontario) with some 60,000 settlers. Nova Scotia was the largest of the maritime provinces, which also comprised New Brunswick, Prince Edward Island, and Cape Breton Island (merged with Nova Scotia in 1820). From 1809, Newfoundland included the mainland coast of Labrador. The huge but unsettled Rupert's Land, North-West Territory, and Oregon Territory – roamed by nomadic Indians – were dotted with trade forts of the Hudson's Bay Company. The western boundary with the United States was extended westward along the 49th parallel in 1818. (National Atlas of Canada, Ottawa)

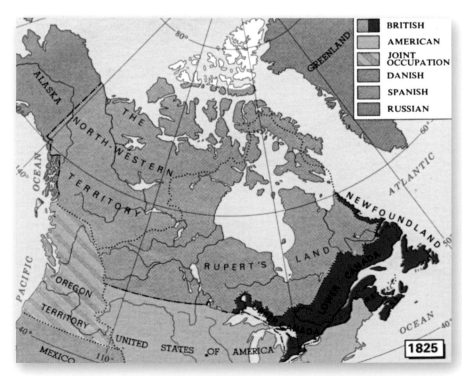

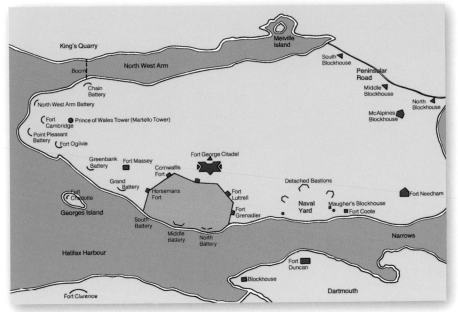

The forts and batteries of Halifax, Nova Scotia. The town had a modest citadel, the earthen Fort George on top of the city's highest hill, but the whole area was dotted by an extensive complex of defenses. The original town was enclosed by a wall with five blockhouses. Later, a succession of batteries and small forts that went from the chain boom blocking naval access to the North West Arm to the Narrows was built. A defense line with blockhouses restrained land access into the peninsula. Martello towers were added from 1796. York Redoubt is not shown as it was farther east (left) of this map. Some of these fortifications continued to be used by the military until the end of World War II. (Private collection)

hovered at about 100,000. Britain was embroiled in an exhaustive world conflict with France's Napoleonic empire for over a decade. It therefore had limited means to fortify and garrison British North America and pursued a policy of minimal, but hopefully effective, fortifications. Royal Engineers were present at Québec and Halifax to maintain the existing military structures in good repair and to lodge the few regular troops assigned to garrison British North America. One advantage it had over the United States was that competent staff work, crucial for strategic planning, went on in Québec, the General Headquarters, and, to a lesser extent, in Halifax. In a general report on defense made by Governor General Sir George Prevost for the Earl of Bathurst in May 1812, stress was laid on the importance of maintaining naval superiority, on the coast and inland, so as to keep communications open and provide means of relief in case of attacks. Forts such as Amherstburg or George were considered "temporary" and Québec City would be qualified as "the only permanent Fortress" of Canada (The National Archives, Colonial Office 42/146). The main concern in fortification was to keep up the existing forts as bases and build a few new ones to secure communications on the western part of the St Lawrence River. Defense otherwise relied on naval squadrons in the North Atlantic and on the inland lakes, with field forces mustered south of Montréal and at the Niagara Peninsula. Thus, owing to naval superiority and a preference for field operations, less emphasis was given to fortifications in Canada than in the United States.

On the Atlantic

The Atlantic provinces relied primarily on the Royal Navy for protection, but there were some fortifications. Newfoundland's garrison had its headquarters at Fort Townshend, a star-plan fort overlooking St John's harbor entrance, as did Fort Amherst with its tower and a battery that had up to 20 guns. This area also had Fort William and Quidi Vidi Battery, the latter of which had four guns. On Signal Hill were the Waldgrave, Queen's, Wallace, Carronade, and Duke of York batteries, of a few guns each, with Chain Rock Battery below, all of which had deterred a French fleet in 1796. The old fort at Placentia

Plan of the Prince of Wales Martello tower, Halifax, Nova Scotia, May 16, 1812. Built on high ground in 1796–97 at Point Pleasant, this tower was the first of almost 200 towers, including five in Halifax, to be built in the British Empire. This one was part of the batteries that formed the first line of the harbor's defenses. From 1802, the upper level had two 24-pdr cannon and four 68-pdr carronades mounted on traversing carriages. The latter were replaced by six 24-pdr carronades in 1808–10. The second story had four 6-pdrs from 1813 as well as barrack accommodations. The ground floor was used for storage. (Library and Archives Canada, Ottawa)

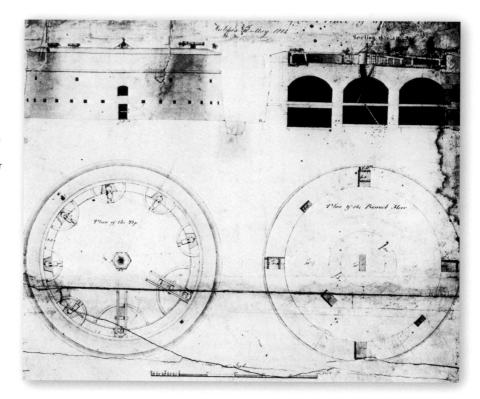

was closed in 1811, but a two-gun earthwork battery was put up in 1813. Prince Edward Island had only the earthwork Prince Edward Battery (built in 1805), mounted with about six guns, guarding Charlottetown's harbor. New Brunswick had a number of blockhouses, notably that of St Andrews, with its earthwork battery with three heavy 24-pdrs. For Tipperary, another earthwork battery was under construction when the war ended. St Andrews was one of the province's garrisoned posts during the war. The main port, St John, had several small works such as the three-gun Dorchester and Graveyard batteries, the five-gun Prince Edward Battery, the six-gun Mortar Battery, the four-gun East Battery, and the two-gun Johnston's Battery. Construction also started in 1813 on the large masonry Carleton Martello tower overlooking the harbor, but it was unfinished and unarmed at war's end.

Halifax, Nova Scotia, lacked a formidable masonry citadel, but the "Warden of the North" did have a very extensive defense complex that covered its peninsula and adjacent shores. Its purpose was to protect the Royal Navy's most important base in North America. The original town, enclosed by a wall with five blockhouse forts, had an earth-and-wood citadel added on top of the city's highest hill. Erosion was soon more effective than a siege and, at the time of the War of 1812, the third version of the citadel, christened Fort George, was built on the hill. It was the 1794–99 "new field work on Citadel Hill," consisting of earthworks faced with planks, around which was a ditch. It had a rectangular plan with two small and two large bastions. Inside were various wooden buildings, including the large Cavalier Barracks that lodged up to 650 men. The fort was armed with some 20 24-pdr cannon and it also had a signal mast. It eventually crumbled and, in 1828, work started on the present masonry citadel that is presently on the site. Halifax's defenses also had a succession of batteries and small forts that went from the chain boom blocking naval access to the North West Arm all

During the War of 1812, Québec City's Hope Gate was one of the two places where one could enter the upper city from the lower town. Although it looks fairly harmless, it is a stone's throw from rampart batteries and other defensive features that would have made any hostile attempt on it next to suicidal. Built in 1786, the gate was destroyed to make way for "progress" in 1873, but has lately reappeared in a most innovative way; as a topiary plant sculpture. This remarkable example put up in 2008 displayed some 30,000 plants of the echeveria (dark grey), alternanthera (green and dark red), and santolia (light grey) varieties. Many North American communities have made outstanding efforts to recreate and preserve historic fortifications, and this is a most imaginative example in the only walled city in North America. (Author's collection)

the way to the Narrows leading into the huge Bedford Basin. A defense line with blockhouses restrained land access into the peninsula. Two additional stone Martello towers were added in 1798–99 and two more in 1812–14. There were no other major forts elsewhere in the province, though many harbors had batteries and blockhouses, and a few had garrisons, such as Fort Edward (Windsor) and Fort Anne (Annapolis Royal). Cape Breton Island was a separate colonial province until 1820, when it merged with Nova Scotia. It had few fortifications: a battery and its blockhouse, each with

View of Québec City, 1818. This was the appearance of the city during the War of 1812. At the left can be seen the fortifications and batteries on Cape Diamond; the building with the flag is the Saint Louis castle (destroyed by fire in 1834), which was the residence of the governor general of British North America. Although often invisible from a distance, the upper edge of the cliff separating the lower town from the upper town was fortified with walls and batteries. These became higher and more visible as the cliff lowered toward the northeast up to Artillery Park (at right) where the Board of Ordnance's headquarters was located, and then joined the landward curtain wall going west. (Print after Lieutenant S. W. L. Stretton, 68th Foot; private collection)

four guns, were at Sydney Mines, two earthwork batteries named Fort Ogilvie were built at Sydney from 1793, and Fort Prince Edward blockhouse was built in 1813 at South Bar.

Lower Canada

Lower Canada (now Québec) had no fortifications on the eastern St Lawrence River until one reached Québec City, the capital of British North America. The Chateau Saint-Louis, originally a French-built fort that included the governor general's palace, had a commanding view over the river and the city. There were batteries near the chateau and at various places on the cliff that separated the upper from the lower city that went from Cape Diamond, the city's highest point, to St John's Gate at the northeast. From there, an earth-and-masonry bastioned curtain wall enclosed the city going

One of the four Martello towers built during 1808–10 on the Plains of Abraham, just west of Québec City's western walls. These acted as an early warning system and forward-defense works. When cleared for action, the roof was removed, revealing artillery on the top of the towers. (Author's collection)

west and then south to Cape Diamond. On the cape itself were batteries and an earthwork citadel. The lower city did not have batteries, nor were there substantial defense works at Lévis on the opposite shore or elsewhere outside the city. As it was, the fortress was considered extremely strong because, like Gibraltar, its natural features made it, with the addition of man-made fortifications, an almost impregnable position. It was "the Key to the whole [of Canada] and must be maintained," Lord Bathurst was advised (The National Archives, Colonial Office 42/146).

Because of this, Québec City as a fortress played a very important part in British military strategy in the War of 1812, which was two-fold. The first was its role as the most secure base where it was possible to receive reinforcements and supplies by the sea and safely ensure their transit into the interior of the country. The second was its crucial role in the strategic plan to be followed if American armies managed to conquer Upper Canada and Montréal. In such an eventuality, the forces would withdraw into Québec City and await seaborne relief. As it was, the fortress was not perfect and needed to be improved. To do so, additional works were decided upon, notably from the plans of Royal Engineers Gother Mann and Ralph Bruyères, who succeeded Mann in 1811. The program concentrated on strengthening the curtain wall facing land, adding outworks to it on the Plains of Abraham, and building a permanent masonry citadel on Cape Diamond. Curtain-wall ditches and ravelins were added in 1807 and four Martello towers were built in 1808–10. The masonry citadel was built too, but after the war, from 1819 to 1832.

Montréal, the largest city in Canada and its business hub, had hardly any fortifications left, its old walls being gradually demolished to make way for

Montréal, Canada's largest city at the eve of the War of 1812. It was the most strategically located business city and, during the war, the target of several American forays that never got close. The old French walls dating from the 1720s, some of which can be seen in the background, were totally inadequate and were slowly demolished between 1803 and 1812. The city's defense depended on a field force permanently posted to the south. Troop reinforcements could be made swiftly, thanks to steamships such as the *Accommodation* seen in the foreground. (Print after A. Sherriff Scott, Musée des Brasseurs du temps, Gatineau, Québec)

RIGHT
Lacolle blockhouse, Lower Canada, built in 1812. It was the scene of an engagement on March 30, 1814, in which an American column marching north into Lower Canada was repulsed, the blockhouse acting as a pivotal feature in the British and Canadian defense. It is now a historic site housing the town of Lacolle's tourism office. (Author's collection)

BELOW
Fort Coteau du Lac, Lower Canada, c.1812–15. This fortification protected one of the most important communication links in Canada, situated west of Montréal on the St Lawrence River. (Model at Coteau du Lac National Historic Site, Parks Canada)

urban development. The strategic plan for its protection depended on a field force permanently stationed on the south shore of the St Lawrence River. Even before war was declared, part of the militia had been mobilized, and such a force was indeed posted from Laprairie to Fort Chambly on the Richelieu River. It was made up of 3,000–6,000 men. The old French fort at Chambly usually served as the field headquarters. Not so much in the fort itself, which was falling to pieces, but in various buildings built near it including a stone military hospital. The redoubts at Isle-aux-Noix near the American border constituted the main fortified stronghold south of Montréal, and its garrison crushed a United States naval attack on June 3, 1813. There was also a blockhouse to the southeast at Lacolle, where American forays were twice repulsed on November 20, 1812, and March 30, 1814.

The most famous action, which saved Montréal, occurred in the woods due south along the Chateaugay River at Allen's Corner, when an American army of some 5,000 regulars under General Wade Hampton marched north, but was beaten back by a small Canadian forward detachment ducking behind trees and abbatis led by Lieutenant-Colonel Charles-Michel de Salaberry on October 13, 1813. A blockhouse was built on the spot in 1814 as a base for Canadian scouts. The western side of Montréal was also vulnerable. To prevent an enemy force from approaching from the west, substantial earthwork fortifications were built in 1813 around the canal and locks that were necessary to enter in order to pass the rapids at Coteau-du-Lac. This consisted of a battery of three 24-pdrs mounted on traversing carriages. An octagonal blockhouse acted as a redoubt and command center.

Upper Canada

Going west on the river, its southern shore was the American state of New York and its northern shore was British Upper Canada. There was no other sizeable fort on the Canadian side until one reached Kingston on Lake Ontario so, in December 1812, Governor General Prevost ordered that one

The fortifications on Isle-aux-Noix. The island's defenses consisted of a fort with two bastion-shaped batteries overlooking both sides of the Richelieu River. These were artillery positions, rebuilt in 1812, which sought to prevent American vessels coming from Lake Champlain to the south (left) from going any farther north. They successfully did this on June 3, 1813, with both United States Navy ships being captured. The naval base on the island, especially its dockyard, was considerably expanded during the War of 1812. (Library and Archives Canada, Ottawa, NMC 17056)

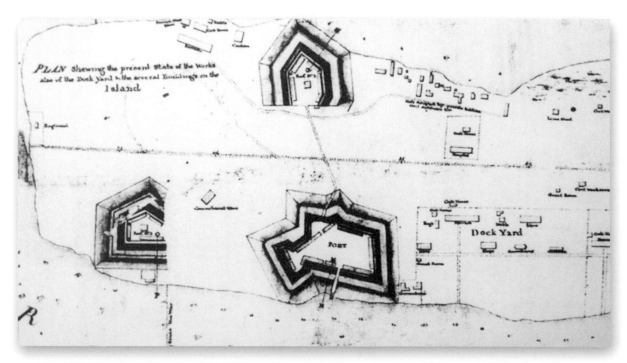

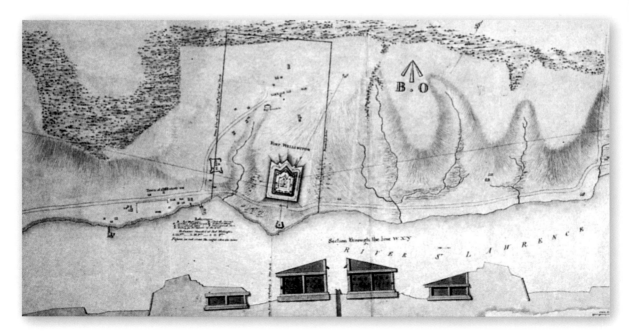

ABOVE

Fort Wellington, built in 1812, guarded the St Lawrence River at Prescott, Upper Canada. This 1816 plan and elevation of this fort shows its appearance during the War of 1812. It was built as a redoubt with a center blockhouse separated by a well, which was at the center of the fort. The elevation shows that this dual blockhouse had a bomb-proofed roof as well as casemate-like galleries below the curtain walls. The structures were made of earth and wood, with some stone foundations. (Library and Archives Canada, Ottawa)

OPPOSITE

Fort York (Toronto), Upper Canada, 1804. Up until its destruction in 1813, Fort York consisted of timber buildings, including a blockhouse, that were enclosed by a stockade. The lakeshore had no defenses. In spite of the fort's minimal fortifications, the garrison put up a spirited resistance in April 1813. (Library and Archives Canada, Ottawa)

be built at Prescott. The militia there had already built a small stockade and a two-gun battery facing the river. The resulting work, built slowly for the next two years, consisted of a one-story blockhouse protected by a high earthwork. It was used as an assembly point for the Canadian attack and capture of Ogdensburg in February 1813. The defeat of Major-General James Wilkinson's army at Chrysler's Farm on November 11, 1813, basically eliminated American military presence on the St Lawrence for the rest of the war. Blockhouses were also built in nearby towns such as Cornwall.

At the time of the War of 1812, Kingston was more of a naval base than "the Fortress of Upper Canada" it later became. The famous citadel of Fort Henry did not exist, though there was a wooden blockhouse built on its site in 1812. Six other blockhouses were also built at that time, following a stockade on the western side with several batteries in present-day downtown Kingston. The most extensive works were at Point Frederick, which had a masonry battery with a blockhouse to protect the nearby Royal Naval Dockyard. A substantial force was in garrison to counter any landing, which was unlikely as long as naval superiority was maintained. The Americans never attacked, considering Kingston to be too well defended. Blockhouses were also built in neighboring communities such as Gananoque, Point Iroquois, and Mallorytown.

The capital of Upper Canada was York (called Toronto since 1834), then a very small town of less than 1,000 residents. However, it was the seat of government and had the province's legislative assembly house and other public buildings. About 500yds to the west was Fort York, which was simply a stockade enclosing barracks with a blockhouse. To the west were earthworks, with Government House and the Western Battery farther out. On April 27, a strong American fleet landed a force of 2,550 men under Brigadier-General Zebulon Pike, which overcame resistance at the outer batteries, but Fort York resisted for about six hours with a garrison of about 800 British, Canadians, and Indians. Their commander, Major-General Sir Roger Sheaffe, ordered his men to evacuate and destroy the fort. As the Americans rushed in, the powder magazine, possibly accidentally ignited prematurely, blew up,

killing six defenders as well as General Pike and wounding or killing some 250 Americans. The enraged Americans went on to destroy Government House, the parliament building, and other public buildings, as well as committing various outrages such as preventing the medical treatment of British and Canadian wounded for two days. This sort of questionable behavior was not forgotten, and retribution came with the burning of Washington's public buildings the following year. The Americans came again on July 31, and burned more public buildings. By the fall, more Royal Navy ships were in the area and earthworks and new buildings were going up. By August 1814, when United States Navy ships wished to raid again, they

ABOVE

Fort Frederick and the Royal Naval Dockyard at Kingston, Upper Canada, *c.*1813. This was the main fortification in Kingston and the most important Royal Navy base on Lake Ontario. (Private collection)

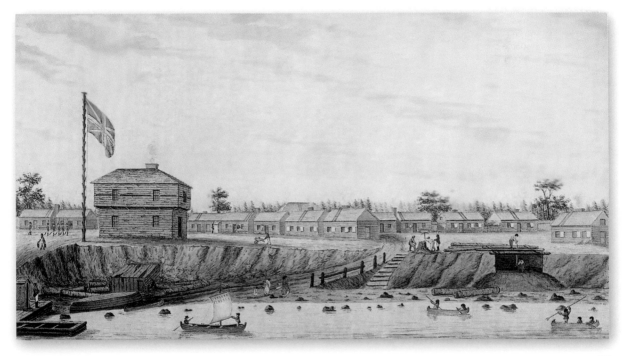

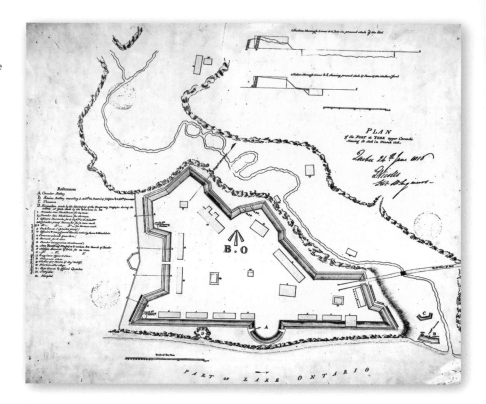

Fort York (Toronto), Upper Canada, 1816. This is the fort as it was after being rebuilt after its destruction during the American attack in April 1813. It featured a circular battery facing Lake Ontario as well as two 18-pdr cannon on traversing carriages in the outside battery to the left. (Plan by Lieutenant-Colonel G. Nicolls, Royal Engineers, March 10, 1816; Library and Archives Canada, Ottawa, NMC23139)

found the place to be too strong and sailed away. The future Toronto recovered quickly and had nearly 10,000 inhabitants by the 1830s.

Canada is separated from the United States by the narrow and wild Niagara River that flows east between lakes Erie and Ontario, first through the mighty Niagara Falls and on below the cliffs of the high escarpment until Lake Ontario is reached. On the American side stands Fort Niagara, which the British occupied until 1796 when, following Jay's Treaty, they moved to Fort George just across the river's estuary. Construction of this earth-and-wood fort went on for several years. It had an elongated design, which gave it a lot of space for its several wooden buildings. Its curtain walls were garnished with several gun positions in its bastions, the widest of these facing the river and the American fort.

F   FORT GEORGE, NIAGARA PENINSULA, 1796–1812

The British forces built Fort George on a rising bluff from 1796 to 1799 to guard the strategically important Niagara River mouth from Lake Ontario. It also protected the maritime installations at Navy Hall on the shore and the village of Newark (now Niagara-on-the-Lake). The fort was the main base of the British forces in Upper Canada and was built as a large irregular rectangle earthwork with six earth-and-wood bastions with a ditch outside and a stockade enclosing the work. A small earth-and-stockade ravelin was outside the fort to protect the gate at the northern end (1). An octagonal blockhouse outside the southern end was connected to the fort by a caponier passage leading to the powder magazine. This blockhouse (2), set in the middle of an enclosed ravelin, was used as an artillery storehouse in peacetime.

The fort's large interior was intended to accommodate many functions (as an artillery park, for example) and could, if the need arose, have more structures. As it was, it contained a spacious and rather attractive officer's mess (3), three barracks built as blockhouses (4), a guardhouse (5), and a stone powder magazine built in a lower dug-out area at the southern end of the fort (6). During the battle of Queenston Heights on October 13, 1812, American gunners bombarding from Fort Niagara across the river scored a direct hit on the magazine's reinforced roof, which started a fire. The 800 barrels of powder within might have exploded, so the fort was quickly evacuated except for a party of local militiamen and Royal Artillery gunners who, led by Royal Engineer Captain Vigoreux, managed to extinguish the flames. This is one of the war's many, if little-known, heroic feats. This large fort was recognized as awkward to defend and, by 1814, had been transformed into a smaller, star-shaped structure.

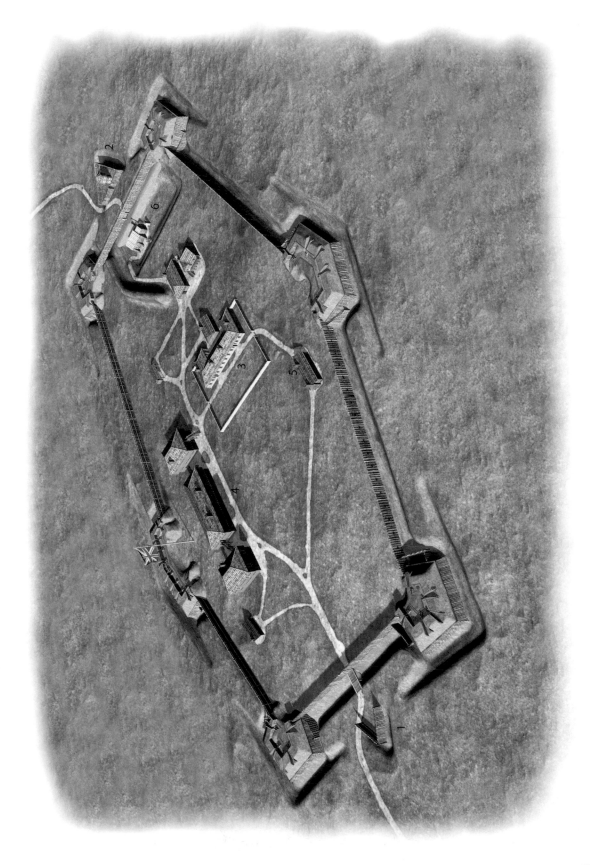

Fort George, Upper Canada, and Fort Niagara, New York, in 1798–99. This plan shows the entrance of the Niagara River with the American Fort Niagara to the south and the British Fort George to the north. (Library and Archives Canada, Ottawa, NMC16811)

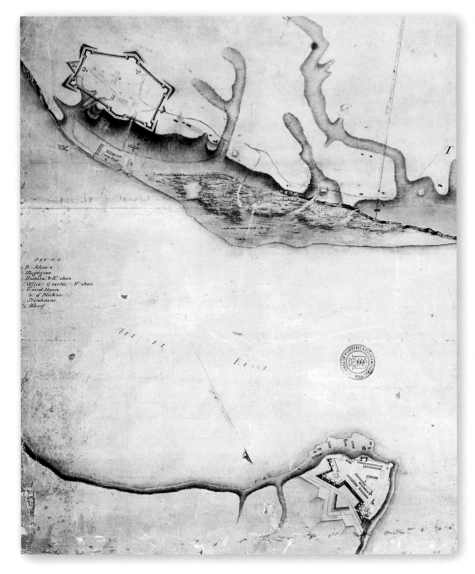

It is said that news of the declaration of war arrived during a dinner given in Fort George by the British officers to the American officers of Fort Niagara, with whom relations were quite friendly. All finished the dinner cordially, said good-bye with wishes for good luck, and the next day they were preparing their cannon. Because of its long shape, the fort was more difficult to defend and made a broad target for enemy guns. Its layout started to be altered in the fall, making it smaller and transforming it into an irregular pentagon with five bastions, but this was a slow process that may not have been finished until 1814. In the meantime, there were artillery duels, and after an epic battle the Americans captured Fort George on May 27, 1813. However, they later suffered defeats outside the fort and, on December 10, 1813, the United States forces evacuated Fort George. It was a cold night, but the bitter American soldiers nevertheless threw the 400 hapless residents of Newark (now Niagara-on-the-Lake) out of their houses, which they then burned. Barely a week later, British and Canadian troops captured Fort Niagara and then proceeded to destroy American homes all the way to Buffalo, after which the futility of such cruel and senseless acts was agreed

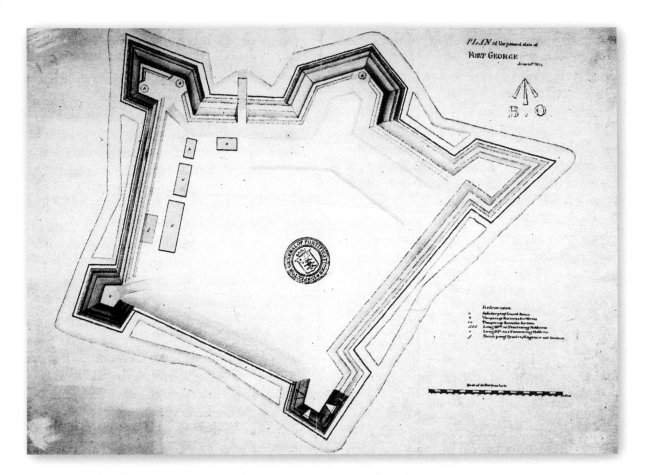

Fort George, Upper Canada, August 1814. This plan shows the new fort's layout following alterations to make it smaller and therefore easier to defend. (Library and Archives Canada, Ottawa, H4/450)

upon by both sides. Reconstruction of Fort George continued, and it had its new shape by the end of 1814.

However, it still had defects regarding its very location, which were addressed first by initially building a small battery at Mississauga Point a short distance to the north. By the summer of 1814 the battery had become Fort Mississauga, which was planned as an irregular star-shaped earthwork redoubt armed with four 24-pdr guns mounted on traversing carriages. Within was a square thick-walled and bomb-proof brick-and-stone tower with rounded corners, probably to deflect enemy fire. There were also several other more perishable buildings that, except for two bomb-proof magazines, could lodge about 80 men. However, its construction had not been finished by the time the war ended. There were otherwise a few isolated blockhouses and small batteries such as Fort Riall, Fort Dummond, Chippawa, Brown's Point, Frenchman's Creek, and the one-gun Vrooman's Battery, which had a role in the battle of Queenston Heights on October 13, 1812. Farther north was the Burlington Heights Depot, which had three lines of earthworks and batteries built in 1813.

At the other end of the Niagara Peninsula was Fort Erie, which was much smaller than Fort George, and facing the American town of Buffalo southwards and Lake Erie westwards. It was built from 1805 on the standard plan of a square with corner bastions, replacing the earlier 1764 stockade fort, which had been partly washed away by the lake's fierce storms. The new fort was sited on higher ground and made of earth faced with masonry, but its construction was interrupted due to budget restraints two years later,

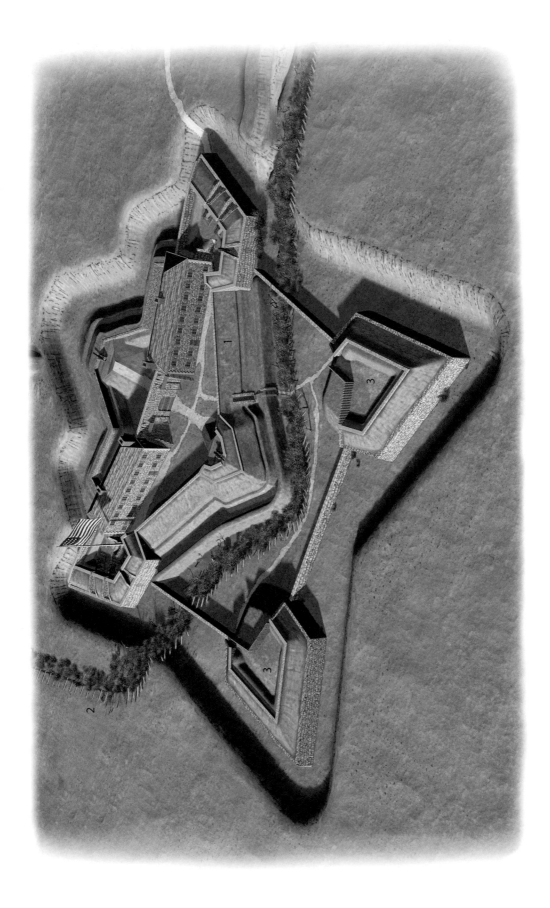

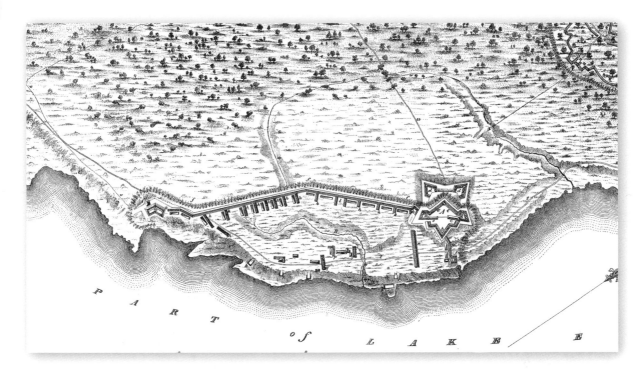

leaving it unfinished. This was somewhat corrected in 1810 with the addition of a wide ravelin on the eastern side. However, by the time war was declared in 1812 the western side remained unfinished, and it could be easily stormed by an enemy force. To provide some protection, a chevron-shaped wall was built in the middle of the fort, which resisted an American assault on November 28, 1812. The fort was subjected to a six-hour bombardment on March 17, 1813. Following the fall of Fort George, Fort Erie was isolated and was ordered evacuated. On May 28, the British spiked the guns and tried to blow up the fort, but it was only partially destroyed. The Americans repaired the work and, in turn, had to abandon the fort in December.

On July 3, 1814, a large American army landed near Fort Erie to attempt yet another invasion of Canada. The fort did not put up an all-out resistance and soon surrendered, much to the displeasure of British commanders, who

Plan of Fort Erie and its associated fortifications at the time of the fierce battles that occurred there in August and September 1814. It was thereafter occupied by Americans. Its line of field fortifications extended west to Snake Hill. (Private collection)

G **FORT ERIE, UPPER CANADA, EARLY AUGUST 1814**

Built from 1805 with the standard plan of a square with four corner bastions and an outside ravelin to protect the gate, Fort Erie had been considerably transformed by 1814. Most frontier forts were made of wood, but the locally available Onondaga flint was used in its construction. Since its western side was not completed when war broke out in 1812, the engineers opted for a radical solution; they built a chevron-shaped curtain wall **(1)** through the middle of the fort in order to enclose it. Outside was a ditch and a line of abbatis **(2)**. The two bastions outside this new line of defense became exterior redoubts **(3)**. It proved to be an effective work, and an American assault force was repulsed there on November 28, 1812. In 1813 the fort was evacuated and reoccupied by the British. It was surrendered without much resistance in early July 1814 to a large American invasion force.

After the battle of Lundy's Lane was fought on July 25, 1814, the US Army retreated to Fort Erie and, from there, built a defensive perimeter that went to Snake Hill and down to Lake Erie, the fort thus becoming the citadel of the US Army's position. The British and Canadian forces now advanced and laid siege to the expanded American position. The key to its capture was to take the fort, but it proved to be a very strong position. The British assault of August 15–16 was repulsed with very high casualties when the northeast bastion's magazine blew up. Our plate shows the fort before that assault. On the other hand, the American sortie of September 17 was equally unsuccessful. The siege was subsequently lifted, but the blockade was kept up. The Americans decided to evacuate their Canadian enclave, since they could not get out of it. On November 5, they blew up Fort Erie. It had been the scene of some of the War of 1812's bloodiest fighting.

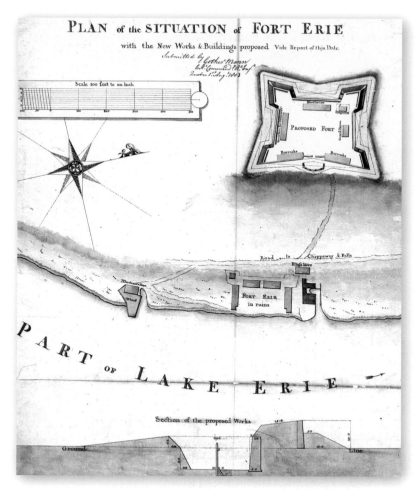

PLAN of the SITUATION of FORT ERIE

with the New Works & Buildings proposed. Vide Report of this Date.

Submitted by Gother Mann
Lt. Col. Commandᵉ R¹ Engⁱ
Quebec 1ˢᵗ Augᵗ 1805

Scale 100 feet to an Inch

PROPOSED FORT

Storehouse

Barracks   Barracks

Road to the Chippeway & Falls

King's Store

FORT ERIE
in ruins

Merchant Store
Wharf

PART OF LAKE ERIE

Section of the proposed Works

Ground   Line

Plan of the "proposed" Fort Erie, Upper Canada, 1805. Royal Engineer Gother Mann's proposal to build a new fort to replace the older fort "in ruins" on the Canadian shore of Lake Erie was approved. It faced the American town of Buffalo, New York. (Library and Archives Canada, Ottawa, NMC3801)

had hoped it would hold out as long as possible in order to delay the Americans. So the Americans advanced, beat a British force at Chippawa on July 5, and were only stopped 20 days later at the hard-fought and bloody battle of Lundy's Lane. The Americans retreated back to Fort Erie, which they transformed into a long fortified field line that went south from the fort to Snake Hill and down to the lake, thus forming an enclave in Canada. Their troops could safely be brought over from Buffalo to try invading Canada yet again. To prevent that, British and Canadian troops blockaded and then besieged this enlarged Fort Erie. On August 15–16 the British assaulted it, but this failed due to the valiant defenders and the explosion of a magazine in the northeast bastion. The British casualties and missing came to over 900 officers and men. The siege nevertheless continued and, on September 17, the Americans attempted a sortie that was beaten back after hard fighting. Four days later the British lifted the siege and moved east to Chippawa, remaining there to intercept any American force that would move farther. In early November, the Americans decided to abandon Fort Erie and cross back into the United States. On November 5 the fort was blown up, this time with success. Only rubble remained.

There was no major post on the Canadian shore of Lake Erie until the Detroit River was reached, facing the United States on its western shore. The British base in the area was Fort Amherstburg (later known as Fort Malden), built after Detroit was evacuated in 1796. It consisted of a large square earthwork with small corner bastions and a ravelin in front of its gate armed with some 15 cannon on its ramparts and three field guns. In 1812 some guns taken at Detroit were added. It was abandoned without a fight after the British defeat at the battle of the Thames, its position having become untenable. The empty fort was occupied by the Americans on September 27, 1813. They started transforming it into a smaller earthwork, which they in turn gave back uncompleted to the British in 1815. There were a few other small works in this area. Bois Blanc near Fort Amherstburg had a blockhouse from 1796. Fort Hope, apparently a small stockade outpost built in 1812, and a small battery faced Detroit across the river at the present Windsor, Ontario. There were also some earthworks built on the September 1813 battlefield of the Thames River (at Dover).

Farther west

The most westerly post garrisoned by regular troops was Fort St Joseph. The fort consisted of a square palisade with small corner bastions of timber located on St Joseph Island, near the northwest shore of Lake Huron and the Sault Sainte Marie channel that led into Lake Superior. It was built in 1796–99 following the garrison's evacuation from Fort Mackinac and abandoned after its garrison had captured and moved back into Fort Mackinac in 1812.

There were many other forts farther west, going all the way to the Pacific coast, but they were trade forts in the networks of the Hudson's Bay and

TOP

Fort St Joseph, c.1799–1812. This fort was built following the evacuation by the British garrison of Fort Mackinac due to Jay's Treaty in 1796. It was an important post for the Indian Department, but Fort Mackinac was more strategically sited and as soon as the British garrison learned that war had been declared they attacked and captured it. (Fort St Joseph National Historic Site, Parks Canada, St Joseph Island, Ontario)

BOTTOM

Fort Astoria, c.1811–15. The American Fur Company built this trade fort in Oregon in 1811. In December 1813 it was occupied peacefully by Royal Navy personnel. It may have had an American flag that was replaced by the Union Jack, but matters were complicated by the fact that the fort and its contents had been sold shortly before to the Canadian North-West Company. (Private collection)

Fort Montgomery, better known as "Fort Blunder." The very odd story of this fort starts in 1816, when the United States proceeded to build a large and powerful casemated octagonal masonry tower. It was to be 30ft high with four levels of casemated batteries, and stand on Rouse's Point at the mouth of the Richelieu River where it flows into Lake Champlain. But construction halted in 1819 when, to their horror, the Americans had to acknowledge that their fort had been built on the Canadian side of the border! Hence its nickname. Following the Webster-Ashburton Treaty of 1842, which granted that parcel of land to the United States, the Americans then decided to build a much larger fort on the spot and construction started in 1844. (Author's collection)

North-West companies. Perhaps the most far-off effect of the War of 1812 occurred at Fort Astoria on the Oregon coast, a palisade work that had been built in April 1811 by American businessman John Jacob Astor's Pacific Fur Company. Two years later, unhampered by the state of war, the American company sold the fort to the Canadian North-West Company. So it seems it was business as usual between American and Canadian fur traders until October 16, 1813, when the British corvette HMS *Racoon* arrived at the fort, seized it, hoisted the Union Jack and renamed it Fort George. There was no fighting; instead, a dinner was given. This capture created the quaint situation where prize money could hardly be paid for seizing British North American property. And when the Stars and Stripes went back up on the flagpole in 1818, ownership remained Canadian. An omen, perhaps, that instead of engaging in futile fighting, Canadians, Americans, and Britons preferred conducting business with each other. This has certainly been the case since the War of 1812 and is quite probably one of that conflict's main lessons.

THE FORTS TODAY

Many forts can be seen today by using the various American or Canadian highway systems. The countryside forts are often on superb natural sites, or on unique parkland in the built-up areas of metropolises such as New York City, Toronto, Boston, or Baltimore. Many of these forts, originally built before the War of 1812, were substantially rebuilt during the 19th century and a few, such as the Boston harbor forts, have emplacements for huge 20th-century guns. Regrettably, of the remarkable Narragansett Bay forts in Rhode Island, only vestiges of Fort Hamilton remain on the largely inaccessible Rose Island, although the later-rebuilt Fort Adams is certainly worth visiting, along with its lovely port city of Newport. In New York City, Castle Williams and Fort Jay still stand on Governors Island while the walls of Castle Clinton can be seen at Lower Manhattan's Battery Park. Baltimore's superb Fort McHenry, maintained by the US Park Service, is very easily accessed by highway, whose exit brings one into a lovely parkland site facing the water. The buildings and armament of the present fort are generally of a period later than the War of 1812, but its ramparts and layout are much the

same as in 1814. The interpretation is focused on the "Star-Spangled Banner" visitor experience, always an emotional moment for Americans. Several War of 1812 forts have been rebuilt in the American Midwest and the huge Fort Meigs is certainly the most impressive of them.

In Canada too, many forts have been altered and/or rebuilt. Such is the case at Halifax where, except for Prince of Wales' Martello tower, the fortifications have been rearmed and added to well into the 20th century. Downtown Québec City is very scenic and full of Old World charm, largely because of its imposing fortifications that are still an integral part of its daily life; its curtain walls look generally the same as they would have in 1812. It is the only remaining city enclosed by a curtain wall in North America; its superb citadel was built after the War of 1812, as were its present large gates. So were most of the splendid fortifications south of Montréal and in Kingston. In Toronto, however, some original structures of the 1812 era remain at Fort

Castle Williams in New York seen from its landward side. This tiered casemate structure has a bastion-like shape at its rear. (Wikimedia)

York, the historic park situated west of the famous CN Tower. On the scenic Niagara Peninsula, Fort George and Fort Erie were reconstructed in the 1930s to look as they did in the 1812 period, and offer excellent interpretive programs. It should be noted that, in Canada, many uniformed staff are not re-enactor volunteers, but paid staff that are professionally trained in visitor services as well as historic maneuvers.

Back on the United states' side of the border, forts Niagara and Mackinac are situated in exceptionally fine sites. Many others forts are in more or less isolated communities that usually have good museums or interpretation centers. On the whole, many happy hours await the visitor of War of 1812 forts and sites.

GLOSSARY OF FORTIFICATION TERMS

Abbatis   A defensive barricade or row of obstructions made up of closely spaced felled trees, their tops toward the enemy and their branches trimmed to points and interlaced where possible.

Banquette   A continuous step or ledge at the interior base of a parapet on which defenders stood to direct musket fire over the top of the wall. A fire-step.

Bastion   A projection in the enceinte, made up of four sides (two faces and two flanks), which better enabled a garrison to defend the ground adjacent to the main or curtain walls.

Berm   A line of wooden stakes or logs, 6–8ft (1.8–2.4m) long, planted in the middle of a ditch and pointing vertically.

Breastwork   *See* parapet.

Casemate   A mortar-bomb or shell-proof chamber located within the walls of defensive works; generally pierced with openings for weapons: loopholes for muskets and embrasures for cannon.

Cordon   The coping or top course of a scarp or a rampart, sometimes of different-colored stone and set proud from the rest of the wall. The point where a rampart stops and a parapet begins.

Counterguard Defensive work built in a ditch in front of a bastion to give it better protection.

Counterscarp The outer side of a ditch or moat. *See* also scarp.

Covered way   A depression, road, or path in the outer edge of a fort's moat or ditch, generally protected from enemy fire by a parapet, at the foot of which might be a banquette enabling the coverage of the glacis with musketry.

Cunette   A furrow located in the bottom of a dry ditch for the purpose of drainage.

Fort York in downtown Toronto (called York until 1834). In the background is the CN tower and the skyline of the city's business district. The infantryman is dressed and equipped as British or Canadian soldiers would have been in 1814–15. (Doug Lavender, Wikimedia)

Curtain	The wall of a fort between two bastions.
Demi-bastion	A half-bastion with only one face and one flank.
Demi-lune	Triangular-shaped defensive work built in a ditch in front of a bastion or of a curtain wall. Also termed a Ravelin.
Ditch	A wide, deep trench around a defensive work. When filled with water it was termed a moat or wet ditch; otherwise a dry ditch or fossé.
Embrasure	An opening in a wall or parapet allowing cannon to fire through it, the gunners remaining under cover. The sides of the embrasure were called "cheeks," the bottom the "sole," the narrow part of the opening the "throat," and the wide part was called the "splay."
En barbette	An arrangement for cannon to be fired directly over the top of a low wall instead of through embrasures.
Epaulement	A parapet or work protecting against enfilade fire.
Fascines	Long bundles of sticks or small-diameter tree branches bound together for use in revetments, for stabilizing earthworks, filling ditches, etc.
Fossé or foss	*See* ditch.
Fraise	A defense of closely placed stakes or logs, 6–8ft (1.8–2.4m) long, driven or dug into the ground and sharpened and arranged to point horizontally or obliquely outward from a defensive position.
Gabion	A large round woven wicker cylinder intended to be set in place and filled with earth, sand, or stones.
Gallery	An interior passageway or corridor that ran along the base of a fort's walls.
Gate	A main entrance into a fortress.
Glacis	A broad, gently sloped earthwork or natural slope in front of a fort, separated from the fort proper by a ditch and outworks and so arranged as to be swept with musket or cannon fire.
Gorge	The interval or space between the two curtain angles of a bastion. In a ravelin, the area formed by the flanked angle and either left open or enclosed.
Guardhouse	The headquarters for the daily guard.

Guérite	A small lookout watchtower, usually located on the upper outer corner of a bastion.
Half bastion	*See* demi-bastion.
Hornwork	A work made up of a bastion front: two half bastions and a curtain wall and two long sides termed branches.
Loopholes	Small openings in walls or stockades through which muskets were fired.
Magazine	A place for the storage of gunpowder, arms, or goods generally related to ordnance.
Martello tower	Small and very solidly built round masonry towers armed with heavy artillery.
Merlon	The solid feature between embrasures in a parapet.
Moat	*See* ditch.
Orgue	*See* portcullis.
Outwork	An outer defense, inside the glacis but outside of the body of the fort. A ravelin is an outwork.
Palisade	A high fence made of stakes, poles, palings, or pickets, supported by rails and set endwise in the ground. *See* also stockade.
Parapet	A breastwork or protective wall over which defenders, standing on banquettes, fired their weapons.
Postern	A passage leading from the interior of a fortification to the ditch.
Rampart	The mass of earth, usually faced with masonry, formed to protect an enclosed area.
Ravelin	An outwork consisting of two faces forming a salient angle at the front and a flank angle to the rear that was usually closed at the gorge. Ravelins were separated from the main body of the place by ditches and functioned to protect curtains. Also called a demi-lune.
Redoubt	An enclosed fortification without bastions.
Revetment	The sloping wall of stone or brick supporting the outer face of a rampart.
Sallyport	A passageway within the rampart, usually vaulted, leading from the interior of a fort to the exterior, primarily to provide for sorties.

Sap	A trench and parapet constructed by besiegers to protect their approaches toward a fortification.
Scarp	The interior side of a ditch or the outer slope of a rampart. *See* also counterscarp.
Stockade	A line or enclosure of logs or stakes set upright in the earth with no separation between them, to form a barrier 8ft high or more. Stockades were generally provided with loopholes. The loopholes were reached by banquettes or elevated walks. *See* also palisade.
Traverse	A parapet or wall thrown across a covered way, a terreplein, ditch, or other location to prevent enfilade or reverse fire along a work.

SELECT BIBLIOGRAPHY

Archives:
The National Archives (Kew, United Kingdom), Colonial Office, and War Office series, maps, and plans.
Library and Archives Canada (Ottawa), maps and plans.
Library of Congress (Washington, DC), manuscripts division, George Washington papers.

Publications:
Aimone, Alan C. and Joseph M. Tatcher, "Three Massachusetts Forts in the War of 1812," *Military Collector & Historian*, Vol. 49, No. 3 (Fall, 1997)
Alcorn, Bill, "Forts on the Niagara Frontier 1679–1963" in *Forts*, Vol. 37 (2009)
American State Papers, Class V: Military Affairs, Washington, DC: United States Congress (1832–61)
Benn, Carl, *Fort York*, Toronto: City of Toronto Culture (2007)
Bonner, William Thompson, *New York: The World Metropolis 1623–1924*, New York: R. L. Polk & Co. (1924)
Brackenridge, H. M., *History of the Late War Between the United States and Britain*, Philadelphia (1839)
Bradford, Robert D., *Historic Forts of Ontario*, Belleville: Mika (1988)
Brown III, William L., *The Army Called it Home*, Gettysburg: Thomas Publications (1992)
Charbonneau, André, *The Fortifications of Isle aux Noix*, Ottawa: Parks Canada (1994)
Charbonneau, André, Yvon Desloges, and Marc Lafrance, *Québec, ville fortifiée du XVIIe au XIXe siècle*, Québec: Pélican (1982)
Davidson, William E., "A Sketch and a Letter for building Forts in the Indian Territory," *Military Collector & Historian*, Vol. 62, No. 2 (Fall, 1997)
Dowart, Jeffery M., *Fort Mifflin of Philadelphia: An Illustrated History*, Philadelphia: University of Pennsylvania Press (1998)
Dunnigan, Brian Leight, *Frontier Metropolis: Painting Early Detroit 1701–1838*, Detroit: Wayne State University Press (2001)
——, *Glorious Old Relic: The French Castle and Old Fort Niagara*, Youngstown: Old Fort Niagara Association (1987)
——, *History and Development of Old Fort Niagara*, Youngstown: Old Fort Niagara Association (1985)
Filion, Mario, *Le blockhaus de Lacolle: Histoire et architecture*, Québec: Ministère des Affaires culturelles (1983)

Jacobs, James Ripley, *The Beginnings of the US Army 1783–1812*, Princeton University Press (1947)

Hall, Jonathan N., *Reconstructed Forts of the Old Northwest Territory*, Westminster, Maryland: Heritage Books (2008)

Hannon, Leslie F., *The Forts of Canada*, Toronto: McClelland and Stewart (1969)

Henderson, Robert, "British Barrack Sleeping Accommodations During the War of 1812," *Military Collector & Historian*, Vol. 61, No. 2 (Summer, 2009)

Lewis, Emmanuel Raymond, *Seacoast Fortifications of the United States: An Introductory History*, Smithsonian Institution: Washington, DC (1970)

Pacey, Elizabeth, *Halifax Citadel*, Halifax: Nimbus (1985)

Piers, Harry, *The Evolution of the Halifax Fortress 1749–1928*, Halifax: Public Archives of Nova Scotia (1948)

Poinsatte, Charles, *Outpost in the Wilderness: Fort Wayne 1706–1828*, Fort Wayne Historical Society (1976)

Reis, Gunter R, "Tower Forts – an overview," *Forts*, Vol. 37 (2009)

Roberts, Robert B, *Encyclopedia of Historic Forts: The Military, Pioneer and Trading Posts of the United States*, New York: Macmillan (1988)

Russel, John, *A History of the United States of America*, Philadelphia: Hogan and Thompson (1814)

Sarty, Roger and Doug Knight, *St John Fortifications 1630–1956*, Fredericton: University of New Brunswick (2003)

Saunders, Ivan J., "A History of Martello Towers in the Defence of British North America 1796–1871," *Canadian Historic Sites: Occasional Papers in History and Archeology*, No. 15, Ottawa: Parks Canada (1976)

Sheads, Scott, R. E. Eshelman, and Donald R. Hickey, *The War of 1812 in the Cheseapeake*, Baltimore: John Hopkins University Press (2010)

Young, Richard J., "Blockhouses in Canada 1749–1841," *Canadian Historic Sites: Occasional Papers in History and Archeology*, No. 23, Ottawa: Parks Canada (1980)

Other:

Pete and Phil Payette have compiled the outstanding "North American Forts" website, which attempts to list every fort since European discovery in North America as well as fortifications elsewhere that have had American garrisons. The result is a truly vast database listing thousands of forts with, for each entry, a short history and, often, links to other sites such as online articles regarding the fort in question. http://www.northamericanforts.com

INDEX

References to illustrations are shown in **bold**. Plates are shown with page in **bold** and caption in brackets, e.g. 24–25 (23).